Series / Number 04-030

Leadership in State Supreme Courts: Roles of the Chief Justice

CRAIG R. DUCAT
VICTOR E. FLANGO
Northern Illinois University

SAGE PUBLICATIONS / Beverly Hills / London

Copyright © 1976 by Sage Publications, Inc.

Printed in the United States of America

All rights reserved. No part of this book may be reproduced
or utilized in any form or by any means, electronic or mechanical,
including photocopying, recording, or by any
information storage and retrieval system, without permission in writing
from the publisher.

For information address:

SAGE PUBLICATIONS, INC.
275 South Beverly Drive
Beverly Hills, California 90212

SAGE PUBLICATIONS LTD
St George's House / 44 Hatton Garden
London EC1N 8ER

International Standard Book Number 0-8039-0542-4

Library of Congress Catalog Card No. 75-9045

FIRST PRINTING

When citing a professional paper, please use the proper form. Remember to cite the correct Sage Professional Paper series title and include the paper number. One of the two following formats can be adapted (depending on the style manual used):

(1) NAGEL, S. S. (1973) "Comparing Elected and Appointed Judicial Systems." Sage Professional Papers in American Politics, 1, 04-001. Beverly Hills, and London: Sage Pubns.

OR

(2) Nagel, Stuart S. 1973. *Comparing Elected and Appointed Judicial Systems.* Sage Professional Papers in American Politics, vol. 1, series no. 04-001. Beverly Hills and London: Sage Publications.

CONTENTS

Introduction 5

Presiding Judges as Small Group Leaders 6

Affective Leadership 9
    Affective Leadership: Chief Justices with Fixed Tenure 13
    Affective Leadership: Role Taking 17
    Affective Leadership: Chief Justices as Minority Leaders 18

Effective Leadership 19
    A Leadership Typology 21
    Judicial Recruitment and Leadership Roles 22

Summary 23

Notes 24

References 24

Appendix A 27

Appendix B: Comparison of State Court Dissent Rates 58

Leadership in State Supreme Courts: Roles of the Chief Justice

CRAIG R. DUCAT
VICTOR E. FLANGO
Northern Illinois University

INTRODUCTION

In terms of influence, the ideal chief justice is a persuasive, esteemed, able, and well-liked judge, who perceives, fulfills, and even expands his role as head of the court.

—David Danelski

This paper will test the expectation that the formal leadership role assumed by the presiding judge of an appellate court modifies his initial voting predispositions. We hypothesize that the managerial abilities of the chief justice will be an important determinant of the level of a court's production and the degree of its cohesion. The thesis that a chief justice, because of his position, has a stake in minimizing court conflict is in accord with conventional wisdom, but runs counter to much of the judicial behavior literature. These studies (Schubert, 1965, 1964, 1959; Sprague, 1968; Spaeth, 1962; Krislov, 1963) have portrayed the presiding judge as responsive to the same stimuli as other court members, voting in accordance with his value preferences when feasible, or motivated by the desire to increase the power of the voting bloc with which he aligns if he is indifferent to the issues under consideration. This paper does not purport to either examine or disprove this coalitional alternative to our thesis. Such a study would entail an examination of opinion assignment behavior and bloc affiliation to ascertain the extent to which the chief justice utilizes such instruments of leadership to achieve coalition policies, rather than institutional objectives.

PRESIDING JUDGES AS SMALL GROUP LEADERS

Much of the work with experimental small groups done by sociologists and political scientists (Asch, 1956; Sherif, 1947; Snyder, 1958; Hare et al., 1965) has relevance for judicial research. Any task-oriented group requires leadership to coordinate group activities and courts are no exception. All small groups possess leaders who maintain an equilibrium between the goal-directed activities of the group and the satisfactions of members of the group. This interactive conception of leadership implies that the group influences the leader as well as being influenced by him.

Courts are primary groups in the sense that they are small enough in size for the members to have direct face-to-face contact over the relatively long period of time that it takes to perform their tasks (Ulmer, 1971; Verba, 1961: 3-16). Whether because of the needs that a group fulfills, the external sanctions that groups place on members, or the internal pressures within the individual to be accepted by the group, particularly an attractive group, it is well established that face-to-face groups exert strong influence over the individual member (Asch, 1951; Festinger et al., 1950; Janis, 1972). Furthermore, group leaders are under more pressure to conform to group standards than are the other members of the group, so that a leader who violates group norms is likely to lose influence as a leader (Verba, 1961: 185-205; Homans, 1950: 141). Leaders are in the peculiar position of being of all individuals the most conforming to group standards—especially since they symbolize and represent the group to the outside world—yet they are different from other group members in terms of influence, and perhaps standards assimiliated in contacts with non-group members. Though judges as a group are thought to be most insulated from outside influence, Henry Glick (1970; Baar, 1970) found that about 60 percent of the state supreme court chief justices who replied to his questionnaire had contacted legislators about specific policy proposals; nearly a quarter had also conferred with the governor, members of his staff, or other executive officials. The advice given by Supreme Court chief justices to the president and members of Congress on legislation affecting the judiciary and on judicial appointments is also well documented (Scigliano, 1971: 62-84; Mason, 1964).

In accord with Ulmer (1963: 15), we assume that leadership is a set of qualities possessed in some degree by all court members, and that leadership will vary with the group situation. This conception of leadership assumes that if the leadership roles are fulfilled, the group process will be characterized by minimum conflict and a rather high degree of social cohesiveness, satisfaction, and productivity (Danelski, 1968). Sidney Verba

(1961: 104) pointed to several studies which found three functional roles common to small groups: a goal-directed role, a group maintenance role, and an individually-oriented role centered around personal recognition and aggression. Like most studies of small groups influenced by Bales and his associates (1950; Slater, 1955), this paper will focus on the first two roles—instrumental and affective leadership, while reserving for later a study of the "outsider" or "maverick" role.

Building on the work of small group theorists, David Danelski (1968) applied these dual leadership roles to the United States Supreme Court. The problem-solving judge, oriented to the instrumental goal of deciding cases, was called the "task leader." In the Bales interaction framework, the task leader is the person who makes the most "suggestions, gives more opinions, orients the discussion more frequently, and successfully defends his ideas more often than the others" (Danelski, 1968: 151). Danelski (1967: 79) suggests his influence may be verified to some extent "by examination of intracourt communications, votes cast and changed, and written opinions circulated and changed at various stages of the decisional process." The social leader, on the other hand, provides the friendliness which makes group relations successful. He raises the self-esteem of members, smoothes over conflicts, eases tensions, accepts suggestions, and, in general, tends to the "emotional needs of his associates" (Danelski, 1968: 152). In their efforts to avoid conflict, social leaders "tend to suppress their disagreements with other justices, i.e., keep it covert—yet rather than withdraw from conflict, they remain in it primarily to restore peace, solidarity, harmony, and friendliness in the Court" (Danelski, 1967: 81). Social leadership is important because a justice who causes resentment within his own group is likely to be ineffective as a leader and thus unable to direct his group to complete the task at hand. Since justices frequently disagree—arguing their cases with the enthusiasm necessary to persuade their undecided or opposing colleagues, the final vote gives rise to tension which "if allowed to get out of hand would make intelligent, orderly decision of cases virtually impossible" (Danelski, 1968: 151).

While one person seldom exercises both leadership roles, the formal leader has a psychological advantage over his brethren in his claim to either or both leadership functions. His position as presiding officer at conferences permits him to state his views first and to select the issues to be discussed. Both Danelski (1968) and McElwain (1949) think that Chief Justice Hughes had the rare combination of abilities necessary to assume both leadership roles. On the other hand, Chief Justice Stone apparently assumed neither of these roles fully; as a result, the cohesion, production, and satisfaction of the court declined markedly. Where a division between task and social leadership does exist, relationships between the two leaders are close, characterized by frequent interaction and agreement (Verba, 1961: 164; Bales and Slater, 1955). Danelski's (1968) description of the relationship between Chief Justice Taft as social leader and his friend, Justice Van Devanter, as task leader supports this expectation in a judicial context.

Although all appellate courts have chief justices, they do not all exercise leadership in the same degree. Moreover, all of the methods used to measure leadership in experimental groups are not appropriate to measuring judicial behavior. The "purple" or "red velour" curtain was designed to protect the sanctity of the conference, and thus the image of judicial objectivity (Miller and Sastri, 1973; Becker, 1966).

One way to determine actual court leadership is to compare the objectives of judicial leadership with the success of the chief justice in attaining them. Danelski (1968: 149) posited successful judicial leadership as achieving such goals as

(1) a majority vote for the chief justice's position,
(2) written opinions satisfactory to him,
(3) social cohesion in the court,
(4) unanimous decisions.

This study will construct a behavioral typology of judicial leadership based upon the last two objectives posited by Danelski.

Data Base

In the construction of a model of chief justice leadership behavior, our analysis will draw upon data from 14 state supreme courts over the 20-year period from 1951-1971. The oft-repeated attribute of the federal system providing "fifty little laboratories" for research is especially relevant to the examination of our thesis. Over a dozen states provide ideal experimental settings for testing our hypothesis—the selection of chief justices by a rotational scheme which enables us to observe a judge's voting behavior before, during, and after his tenure as chief justice.

Anticipating the criticism that the courts selected for analysis—though providing the acid test for the thesis—do not include judiciaries with high dissent rates, we have added California, Michigan, New York, and Pennsylvania to our sample to provide a control group. However, since the tenure of the chief justice in these four states is coterminus with the remainder of his service on the court, the control group will only provide a test for the "before-during" phase of the hypothesis. In addition, the supreme courts of New Jersey and Wisconsin were included in the sample to enhance comparability with other judicial studies.

A "court" is defined by the tenure of its chief justice. Usually, states which provide for a rotating chief justiceship also specify a fairly short term of office. This means that states using a rotation scheme for selecting their chief justices have many more courts (an average of 7.7 per state) than do states which do not use a rotational scheme (an average of 2 per state during the period of analysis). As a result, trends found in states without a rotational plan for selecting chief justices—that is the control group—may be obscured unless analyzed separately.

Although we attempted to be consistent with current terminology, it is necessary to distinguish the dissent rate of *courts* from that of *judges*. The dissent rate of a court is defined as the proportion of the nonunanimous decisions divided by the total number of decisions rendered by the court, while the dissent rate of the judge is the number of times an individual justice dissented divided by the number of nonunanimous decisions in which he participated.

Appendix A gives the dissent rates of both courts and judges for the 20-year period under analysis. Appendix B lists a comparison of our dissent rate for courts with the dissent rates reported by Canon and Jaros (1969) in their survey covering the 1961-1967 period and by Glick and Vines (1973) conducted in 1966. The similarity between our findings, based on a universe of cases, and those determined by Canon and Jaros is testimony to the fact that their well-executed sampling technique is more accurate in estimating the overall dissent rate of courts than the one-year computation of all cases such as Glick and Vines made. Even the discrepancies between the data reported in this paper and those reported by Canon and Jaros can easily be accounted for by changes in dissent rates which occurred outside the restricted time frame of their analysis.

AFFECTIVE LEADERSHIP

Small group research indicates that there may be a trend towards unanimity in small groups.

> Decisions in small face-to-face groups ... are often made on the basis of formal vote and majority rule. In a small face-to-face group made up of peers and relatively isolated from external pressures there may well be a single group goal or a single means to that goal that is in the best interests of all members [Verba, 1961: 222].

Consensus decision-making under conflict-free conditions may indeed be the relevant model for most judicial decision-making situations. As Ulmer (1971: 13) contends, "An obvious fact about collegial courts is that they tend strongly not only toward conformity, but also toward unanimity." This assertion is given empirical support by the research of Canon and Jaros (1969) who found that of their sample of 56 state supreme courts, 32 had unanimity rates about 90 percent and 44 courts rendered unanimous decisions more than 80 percent of the time.[1] The traditional explanation for the absence of deviance is that "dissent detracts from the prestige of the court and undermines its institutional solidarity" (Ulmer, 1971: 13). Dissent, so the argument goes, not only creates uncertainty in the law, but also reduces the impact of judicial decisions (Glick, 1971: 95). As Murphy (1962) put it, "since a five-four decision may serve to emphasize the unsettled nature of the doctrine involved, and so encourage opposition to it, a justice has a strong incentive to secure more than a simple majority acquiescence." While most justices may be concerned with presenting a facade of legal consensus to the world, there are some—like the justice for whom dissenting is distasteful because it is an explicit, direct criticism of his colleagues' work—who are more concerned with the effects of dissents within courts (Glick, 1971: 97).

Most justices desire to increase the impact of their decisions and to avoid the adverse effects of visible conflict. Other things being equal, they would prefer unanimous decisions. Furthermore, the influence of the chief justice, combined with court tradition, discourages dissenting opinions. J. Woodford Howard (1968) gives several examples of the sacrifice of deeply-held views to group and institutional interests. McElwain (1949) reports that Chief Justice Hughes attempted to achieve as great a degree of unanimity as possible without compromising the integrity of the majority opinion. And Taft considered all but the most principled dissents as placing personal vanity above institutional loyalty (Danelski, 1961: 184). Said Taft, "A Justice whose dissents become levers for legislative or administrative action reversing judicial policies may come to be regarded as disloyal to the bench" (Murphy, 1964: 61). It seems logical to conclude that a chief justice would feel more of an obligation than his colleagues to protect institutional stability by curbing his tendencies to dissent and agreeing with the majority whenever possible. An important consideration of judges interviewed by Glick (1971: 115) in assessing the influence of the chief justice was his position as official head of the state judicial system. The results of the Atkinson and Neuman study (1969), though covering a limited time period, tend to confirm the hypothesis that the chief justice votes to protect the court as an institution. Although all justices pay a "cost" for voting contrary to the majority, it seems to us that the chief justice has a particularly strong stake in defending his institution and in avoiding isolation from other judges. Only an issue of significant ideological importance should convince him to maintain his own individuality rather than to go along with the majority.

Our general hypothesis is, then, that the chief justice, as formal leader of a state supreme court, is an important influence in the degree of consensus achieved by his court. We expect the concern of the chief justice for institutional stability to lead to his promotion of unanimity wherever possible. Toward this end, he may suppress his own tendencies to dissent even if the decisions go contrary to his own value preferences. A clear example of this behavior, given by Danelski (1967: 78), is the change in dissent behavior of Chief Justice White. As associate justice he averaged about ten dissents per term, but as chief justice his dissent rate fell to about four dissents per term. We feel that concern for affective leadership, as manifested in lower rates of dissent—regardless of the types of issues presented for decision—will account for the behavior of the chief justice even when differences in court size and political complexion are held constant.

A corollary to this hypothesis is anticipated in view of the Atkinson-Neuman finding that judges vote to protect the integrity of their doctrinal convictions. If the dissent rate of the chief justice does not decrease during his term of office, we would expect it is because of his differing, and deep, ideological commitments. Our crude, but reasonable and often used index of ideological affinity is political party affiliation (Shapiro, 1968; Schubert, 1959: 129-142; Ulmer, 1962; Nagel, 1961; Adamany, 1969; Bowen, 1965; Danelski, 1969). A chief justice who belongs to a different political party than a majority of justices on his court can be expected to register a higher dissent rate than would otherwise be expected of a judge in his position.

Before testing the hypothesis that dissent rates of judges will decline when they become chief justices, it is necessary to show that persons selected as chief justices are not different from their colleagues in the sense that they are already "team players" with low dissent rates. To do this, we have adopted Stuart Nagel's (1969: 177) method of comparing dissent rates of judges from different states by noting whether or not they were above or below the collegial mean. Table 1 shows the results of this analysis. Table 1 illustrates that the chief justice has no statistically significant ($P = .05$) tendency to be below the average dissent rate of all judges serving on his court. Therefore, the expected decline in a judge's rate of dissent when he becomes chief justice can not be attributed to the consistent selection of low dissenters to be presiding judges.

TABLE 1
The Dissent Rate of Chief Justices Contrasted with that of Associate Justices in States Possessing a Rotational Scheme of Leadership and in Control States

Control States

	Above Judges' Average	Below Judges' Average	N
Chief Justices	2	10	12
Associate Justices	42	63	105
	44	73	117

$X^2 = 2.498$ P. = .12

States with Rotational Scheme

	Above Judges' Average	Below Judges' Average	N
Chief Justices	37	40	77
Associate Justices	238	186	424
	275	226	501

$X^2 = 1.71$ P. = .19

TABLE 2
Change in Dissent Rates of Justices in Courts with High Dissent Rates (Life Tenure)

	Dissent Rate		
	Increases	Decreases	N
Chief Justices	1	7	8
Associate Justices	23	16	39
	24	23	47

$$x^2 = 5.7 \quad P. = .02$$

As indicated above, justices from the high dissent states forming our control group do not remain on the bench after their tenure as chief justice is completed; therefore, only a comparison between a judge's dissent rate before and during his tenure as chief justice is possible in those states. The difference between an individual's dissent rate as court member and as chief justice is one situation and one opportunity to test the thesis. The comparatively long tenure of judges in the control group reduces the number of situations in which our hypothesis can be tested, but this also makes the tests more reliable since the dissent rates are based upon very large numbers of cases.

Table 2 shows that individual dissent rates fell for justices who became chief justice, while rising for colleagues who did not. This evidence is strong support for our thesis that justices, upon assuming office as chief justice, will curb their tendencies to dissent. This table, of course, does not purport to measure the magnitude of the rise or fall in dissent rate, merely whether it was higher or lower than in the previous court when these judges were not constrained by the extra responsibilities of the chief justiceship.

AFFECTIVE LEADERSHIP: CHIEF JUSTICES WITH FIXED TENURE

States in which the chief justice serves a fixed term of office should provide a more stringent test for the thesis because dissent rates can be recorded *after* a justice completes his term as presiding officer of the court. If our theisis is correct, once freed from the constraints of the chief justice role, a judge's dissent rate will increase, although perhaps not as much as it was before he assumed the chief justiceship.

Table 3 shows that the dissent rates of chief justices with fixed terms of office decrease upon assuming office and in this way behave like chief justices with life tenure (Table 2). This result partially confirms our thesis. However, we had expected the dissent rate of the chief justice to rise after he left office, regardless of the trend in dissent adopted by the court as a whole. Although the dissent rates of the chief justices did increase overall, there was no significant difference between their dissent rates and those of other justices sitting with them on the bench.

In one sense, this is a better statement of our thesis than our original hypothesis: upon assuming office, the dissent rate of the chief justice will decrease, but upon relinquishing his office the dissent rate of the chief justice will be indistinguishable from that of his fellow associate justices.

Justices from South Dakota and Illinois were excluded from the above analysis because the very short terms of office for chief justices in those states, combined with the low dissent rates, produced a high percentage of unanimous decisions in each court. Rather than contaminate the data in Table 3 with less reliable data, these findings are reported separately. Percentages in some instances were based upon fewer than ten cases and so a change in one vote would greatly influence the dissent rate of a justice. On the other hand, we felt it was necessary to include in our sample of courts with rotating chief justiceships, these courts with short, fixed terms of office in the event that the short term of office modifies the chief justice role.

Courts in which the tenure of the chief justice is comparatively short do not follow the pattern of dissent behavior evidenced in the other courts studied. Although the dissent rate of justices assuming the chief justiceship decreased more often than not, the number of chief justices whose dissent rate decreased was not significantly different from the number of associate justices whose dissent rate also decreased with the change in leadership.

It appears that the number of justices who manifest social leadership by sharply reducing the number of their own dissents is most pronounced when the formal leadership role is accepted for life. A significant decrease in dissent rate is noticeable in courts where the tenure of the chief justice is fixed, but not for life. The drop in dissent rate of the chief justice is not significant in courts that provide for the frequent turnover of chief justices. It may be that role constraints are more effective—both for the chief justice himself and for the attitude of his colleagues toward him—if the role is permanent, less effective if the leadership role is fairly long, and least effective if the chief justice and his colleagues realize that another member will be presiding the following year. Whether this is so because a justice with short tenure just does not consider himself a chief justice or

TABLE 3

Changes in Dissent Rates of Chief and Associate Justices in States Providing
Long Terms of Office for the Chief Justice

Change in Dissent Rate[a]

	After Assuming Office			After Leaving Office		
	Increases	Decreases	N	Increases	Decreases	N
Chief Justices	28	40	68	26	15	41
Associate Justices	221	181	402	168	150	318
	249	221	470	194	165	359
	$X^2 = 4.44$	$P. < .05$		$X^2 = 1.64$	$P. = .20$	

[a] Justices participating in fewer than 10 nonunanimous decisions were excluded from this table.

TABLE 4

Change in Dissent Rates of Chief and Associate Justices in South Dakota and Illinois. Effects on Dissent Rate of Short Terms of Office for the Chief Justice

Change in Dissent Rate

	After Assuming Office			After Leaving Office		
	Increases	Decreases	N	Increases	Decreases	N
Chief Justices	14	18	32	12	16	28
Associate Justices	75	67	142	64	60	124
	89	85	174	76	76	152
	$X^2 = 0.83$	P. = .39		$X^2 = 0.70$	P. = .41	

because the acceptance of a leadership role takes time to have an impact on behavior can not be determined from this type of analysis. What we can say is that Tables 2, 3, and 4 illustrate the tendency, certainly, of the chief justice's dissent behavior to differ from that of his colleagues.

AFFECTIVE LEADERSHIP: ROLE TAKING

A test of the original thesis under more dynamic conditions would require the dissent rates of the chief justices to be compared through time. Eliminating the stability situation from Galtung's "ISD" trichotomy curves (1967: 236-238) leaves four longitudinal patterns of dissent. The first transition point denotes the change in dissent rate between the time a justice served on the court as an associate justice and the time he served as chief justice. The second transition point represents his change in dissent rate from the time he served as chief justice to the time he returned to the position of associate justice. A combination of these two transition points yields four distinct patterns of dissent. Pattern 1 is a condition of continuously rising dissent rates and pattern 4 is the opposite condition of a steadily decreasing rate of dissent. Only pattern 3 supports the hypothesis as originally stated. Of the 70 chief justices on whom data were available on *both* transition points, 27 evidenced dissent behavior which would tend to support our thesis and 15 revealed a pattern of dissent (pattern 2) which ran directly counter to our hypothesis. Patterns 1 and 4 are partial confirmations of the thesis in that the dissent pattern of the chief justice conformed to the expected configuration on one of the transition points but not the other (see Table 5).

TABLE 5
Change in Dissent Rates of Justices Before, During and After Their Tenure as Chief Justice

First Transition Point (Change in Dissent rate after assuming office)		Second Transition Point (Dissent rate after leaving office)		N
		Increases	Decreases	
	Increases	1 — 12	2 — 15	27
	Decreases	3 — 27	4 — 16	43
				70

*Indicates tenure as chief justice.

TABLE 6
Effects of the Chief Justice Role on Dissent Behavior

Dissent Rate	All chief justices	Chief justices with long terms of office
Increases	42	29
Decreases	68	48
	110	77

In view of our earlier finding that the dissent rate of the chief justice may *either* increase or decrease upon leaving his position, but will nevertheless be indistinguishable from that of his colleagues, we decided that the second transition point is really not crucial, and perhaps not even relevant, to our thesis. Regardless of his pattern of dissent after a chief justice becomes an associate justice once again, since it will be indistinguishable from that of his fellow associate justices, his rate of dissent must decrease upon assuming the chief justiceship to provide evidence that the formal leadership role does indeed impose an observable constraint on voting. By adopting this modified hypothesis, more data become available to test the thesis. Dissent rates of chief justices not included in Table 5 because data on the second transition point were not available—either because the chief died in office, retired upon completing his term, or possessed life tenure in the first place—can now be considered.

Table 6 shows that chief justices, more often than not, did dissent with less frequency when they were in office than they did before assuming the chief justiceship. Every chief justice in Pennsylvania, California, Nevada, and New Jersey had a lower rate of dissent while chief justice than he had as an associate justice. On the other hand, 42 of the 110 justices undergoing analysis possessed higher rates of dissent as chief justice than they had before taking office. Even discounting judges from Illinois and South Dakota, states which have extremely short terms of offices for their chief justices, 29 out of 77 justices had higher rates of dissent as chief justice than they had before assuming that office.

AFFECTIVE LEADERSHIP: CHIEF JUSTICES AS MINORITY LEADERS

Our corollary hypothesis would lead us to expect that in those instances where the chief justice does not conform to the expected pattern, he is voting in accordance with deeply-held ideological positions. A chief justice

TABLE 7
Relationship Between the Dissent Rate of the Chief Justice and the Partisan Composition of the Court

	Dissent Rate		
	Increases	Decreases	N
Party of the Chief Justice			
Majority party	14	29	43
Minority party	6	4	10
	20	33	53

$x^2 = 2.6 \quad p. < .10$

whose party affiliation differs from that of the majority of the judges sitting on his bench may be an isolate or merely a member of a minority bloc, regardless of his formal leadership position. We were not able to test this proposition fully because exactly half of these deviant dissent patterns occurred in three states (South Dakota, Oklahoma, and Florida) where party affiliation could not be used as an indicator of ideology since nearly all of the judges are affiliated with one political party. Perhaps a more comprehensive understanding of the political situation in each of these three states would enable us to distinguish factions in the one-party states, much as Schubert (1959: 129-142) distinguished "old line" from "Williams" Democrats in Michigan. This paper, however, is restricted to an analysis of ideology dependent upon partisan affiliation, although we realize that more complex indicators of ideology, such as content analysis, may resolve this dilemma (Kort, 1962; Danelski, 1966). Party affiliations of justices on nearly all of the courts in the remaining six states were obtained and Table 7 shows the results of the tabulation. Parisan affiliation of the chief justice vis-à-vis the affiliations of other court members does not contribute as much to the explanatory power of the thesis as we had first thought.

EFFECTIVE LEADERSHIP

Until now, we have discussed the affective or social leadership role of the chief justice. Yet Glick (1971: 116) in his interviews with supreme court justices in four states reports that most chief justices were perceived as being task-oriented: "In terms of its effects on the decision-making process, the most important source of the chief justice's influence is task leadership." This should not be surprising given the position of the chief justice as titular head of the court, chief administrative officer, and representative to outside groups. He is responsible for coordinating the activities of his colleagues, which means that he is usually better informed about overall court operations than his brethren and may mean that he has additional administrative resources, such as an extra clerk. In a majority of collegial courts in the United States, the chief justice makes opinion assignments (Ulmer, 1971: 21). The power of opinion assignment is important in state supreme courts for many of the same reasons that it is important in the United States Supreme Court: it may determine the value of a decision as precedent, it may make the decision more or less acceptable to the general public, it may hold together the chief justice's majority when the vote is close, and it may persuade dissenting judges to join in the opinion (Danelski, 1968: 156). Furthermore, a chief justice who is generous, considerate, and impartial in his opinion assignments will tend to be well-liked by his associates and thus be in a good position to exercise social leadership (Danelski, 1961: 170).

An adept chief justice should be able to use his institutional resources in combination with his personal skills to reduce, not only his own dissent rate, but the dissent rate of his court as well. Therefore, the *change* in the ratio of nonunanimous to unanimous decision that occurs during the tenure of a particular chief justice will be our measure of effective or task leadership. Note that this measure is based upon Danelski's fourth objective of judicial leadership—unanimity. While recognizing that the dissent rate of the court is not completely under the control of the chief justice and that other structural and organizational factors, such as the number of judges on the court or the presence or absence of an intermediate appellate court (Fair, 1971), may influence the dissent rate of the court, nevertheless we do not expect that this dissent rate would increase during the tenure of an effective chief justice. Note that we are not comparing dissent rates *among* courts in the different states—which, of course, vary according to the peculiar economic, political, and social conditions in each state—but *change* in dissent rates of courts *within* a single state, which should not be subject to these kinds of fluctuations. A glance at the data presented in Appendix A or that presented by Glick and Vines (1973: 80) will soon convince the reader that there is no general trend for the dissent rate of courts to either form a pattern of increase or decrease over time.

A LEADERSHIP TYPOLOGY

If changes in the dissent rates of chief justices and their courts are indeed useful measures of social and task leadership, perhaps they can be combined to form an empirically based typology of judicial leadership. The resulting typology seems to be a reasonable classification of judicial leadership and does satisfactorily comport with Danelski's examples of leadership behavior on the U.S. Supreme Court. Extraordinary leadership should result in decreasing dissent rates for both the chief justice and for the court as a whole, whereas an increase in both types of dissent suggests a deficiency in leadership skills. The situation where the dissent rate of the chief justice decreases while the dissent rate of the court increases suggests leadership by example—social leadership. The social leader may find it easier to curb his own propensity to dissent than to risk the loss of affection of his associates by presenting forceful arguments on the merits of the case. The task leader, on the other hand, being more concerned with decisional outcomes than the personal feelings of his colleagues will attempt to persuade his fellows vigorously, if necessary, to win his point.[2]

Still, we are not altogether comfortable with the definition of task leadership that would have the dissent rate of the court decreasing without the chief justice himself restraining his propensity to dissent. Interestingly enough, Professor Danelski (1968), while providing examples of chief justice as non-leader (Stone), social leader (Taft), and extraordinary leader (Hughes), did not provide an example of a case in which the chief justice was the task leader.

One possible explanation for this peculiar behavior of the task leader, as defined in Table 8, may lie in his leadership style. As Glick (1971: 89) points out, there are several techniques for handling differences on collegial courts, but persuasion, compromise, and voting seem to be the most prevalent on state supreme courts. It may be that certain of these tech-

TABLE 8
Meshing the Empirical Indicators of Judicial Leadership

Affective Leadership		Effective Leadership (Dissent rate of the Court)	
		Increases	Decreases
(Dissent rate of the Chief Justice)	Increases	Non-leader	Task leader
	Decreases	Social leader	Extraordinary leader

niques are more amenable to different types of leaders. For example, the give and take of a compromise solution would seem most appropriate for social leaders, whereas voting, without much of an effort to persuade or to compromise with other justices, would seem to be the hallmark of the non-leader. The task leader, it seems to us, would choose persuasion as the means to resolve disputes, and indeed the very definition of a task leader would seem to imply a person taking the initiative, vigorously presenting his position on the merits of the case (Danelski 1967: 80). This tactic may be successful in cases where opposition justices do not feel strongly about the issue under discussion or where the chief justice has a commanding presence; in this event unanimous decisions may result. In cases where a deep ideological gulf separates justices, the court is likely to become polarized. If this happens the vigorous presentation of the issues by the chief justice may stimulate a greater cohesion among his opponents. Under these conditions, if the chief justice were outvoted it would be awkward for him to join the majority he so strongly opposed. In this manner, the dissent rate of the court could decrease, while the dissent rate of the chief justice would increase. Since task leaders, because of their production-orientation, are not usually well-liked, though they may be highly respected, this explanation is plausible. However, more research focusing upon opinion assignments and voting blocs within courts whose formal leader is also a task leader is required to confirm this suspicion.

JUDICIAL RECRUITMENT AND LEADERSHIP ROLES

As a footnote to this discussion, Glick (1971: 117) notes that it would be difficult to exercise task leadership in Pennsylvania because of the high degree of political conflict involved in judicial elections. Chief Justice Bell, presiding at the time of the Glick survey, is considered to be a social leader in our scheme. By contrast, Glick concluded that New Jersey's Chief Justice Weintraub, an extraordinary leader by our standards, was a task leader. This comparison can not be extended further because Glick's (1971: 117) survey was not able to find one chief justice who performed a social leadership function.

However, Glick's contention that there was a relationship between political conflict in recruitment and the exercise of task leadership in the courts aroused our interest because in that event the method of recruitment might provide a cue to leadership roles of chief justices. Table 9 tests this hypothesis with our data.

Although no striking trends are evident in Table 9, it does appear that non-leader chief justices are most likely to be found in states selecting

TABLE 9
Judicial Recruitment and Leadership Roles

Method of Recruitment[a]	Leadership Roles			
	Extraordinary	Task	Social	Non-leader
Partisan election	7	10	12	3
Missouri Plan	10	5	7	3
Non-partisan election	10	10	14	10
N	27	25	33	16

[a]The one state (New Jersey) selecting judges by appointment provided only one leadership situation, and that justice (Weintraub) was an extraordinary leader.

judges by means of nonpartisan election. States with a high degree of political conflict associated with judicial selection, namely states which use partisan election as their method of recruitment, seem to obtain a number of both task and social leaders.

SUMMARY

While we found no strong correlation between method of selection and leadership role, we have developed an empirically-based typology of judicial leadership that makes it possible to compare leadership roles among justices in different states. Validation of this technique within particular states by comparing the results of this analysis with the results of opinion assignment analysis and bloc analysis is the next logical step. It may even be possible to refine our measures of judicial leadership by using the magnitude of the change in dissent rates for both the chief justice and the courts. If this typology is found to articulate well with reality—rather than relying upon essentially intuitive case studies, based upon private correspondence, interviews, and other difficult to obtain data—we will have developed a method of measuring judicial leadership that is both independent of the researchers conducting the studies and also truely comparative.

NOTES

1. More than 50 courts are reported here because some states divide their highest tribunals into criminal and civil jurisdictions. Canon and Jaros counted these courts separately.

2. For comparable, and indeed parallel leadership typologies, see particularly Koontz and O'Donnell (1962: 582). An illustration of the psychological underpinnings of these typologies was suggested by Horney (1937, 1945, 1950) and analogized to legislative and executive office holders by Barber (1965, 1972) and to Supreme Court justices by Danelski (1967). In a personal communication dated December 16, 1974, Danelski outlined these parallel relationships to us:

Horney	Barber (1965)	Barber (1972)
Compliant	Spectator	Passive-positive
Aggressive	Advertiser	Active-negative
Detached	Reluctant	Passive-negative
Adjusted*	Lawmaker	Active-Positive

*Horney does not use the term "adjusted," but the type is clearly implied in her work. Danelski (1967: 84) used this label in describing Chief Justice Marshall.

We are particularly intrigued by the correspondence between social leaders and the passive-positive personality type, although direct comparisons are virtually impossible because only Taft was both a president and a Supreme Court justice. Both Danelski (1967: 81-82) and Barber (1972) lend support to this observation by discussing Taft using essentially the same typology.

REFERENCES

ADAMANY, D. W. (1969) "The political party variable in judges' voting: conceptual notes and a case study." Amer. Pol. Sci. Rev. 63: 57.

ASCH, S. (1956) "A minority of one against a unanimous majority." Psychological Mono. 70.

--- (1951) "Effects of group pressure on modification and distortion of judgment," in H. Guetzkow (ed.) Groups, Leadership and Men. Pittsburgh: Carnegie Press.

ATKINSON, D. N. and D. A. NEUMAN (1969) "Toward a cost theory of judicial alignments: the case of the Truman bloc." Midwest J. of Pol. Sci. 13 (May): 271-283.

BAAR, C. (1970) "The growth of federal judicial administration structures." Presented at the Midwest Pol. Sci. Assn. meeting, Chicago.

BALES, R. F. and P. SLATER (1955) ch. 7 in T. Parsons and R. F. Bales (eds.) Family, Socialization and Interaction. Glencoe: Free Press.

BARBER, J. D. (1972) The Presidential Character. Englewood Cliffs: Prentice-Hall.

--- (1969) "The president and his friends." Presented at the Amer. Pol. Sci. Assn. meeting, New York.

--- (1965) The Lawmakers. New Haven: Yale Univ. Press.

BECKER, T. L. (1966) "Surveys and judiciaries, or who's afraid of the purple curtain." Law and Society Rev. I: 133-143.
BOWEN, D. R. (1965) "The explanation of judicial voting behavior from sociological characteristics of judges." Ph.D. dis. New Haven: Yale University.
CANON, B. C. and D. JAROS (1969) "State supreme courts—some comparative data." State Government 42 (Autumn): 260-264.
DANELSKI, D. J. (1969) "Notes for further research," pp. 397-403 in G. Schubert and D. Danelski (eds.) Comparative Judicial Behavior. New York: Oxford Univ. Press.
——— (1968) "The influence of the chief justice in the decisional process of the supreme court," pp. 147-160 in T. Jahnige and S. Goldman (eds.) The Federal Judicial System. New York: Holt, Rinehart & Winston.
——— (1967) "Conflict and its resolution in the supreme court." J. of Conflict Resolution 11 (March): 71-86.
——— (1966) "Values as variables in judicial decision-making: notes toward a theory." Vanderbilt Law Rev. 19 (June): 721-740.
——— (1961) "The influence of the chief justice in the decisional process," in W. F. Murphy and C. H. Pritchett (eds.) Courts, Judges, and Politics. New York: Random House.
——— (1961) "The chief justice and the supreme court." Ph.D dis. Chicago: Univ. of Chicago.
FAIR, D. (1971) "State intermediate appellate courts: an introduction." Western Pol. Q. 24: 415-424.
FESTINGER, L. S. SCHACTER and K. W. BLACK (1950) Social Pressures in Informal Groups. New York: Harper.
GALTUNG, J. (1967) Theory and Methods of Social Research. New York: Columbia Univ. Press.
GLICK, H. R. (1971) Supreme Courts in State Politics. New York: Basic Books.
——— (1970) "Policy-making and state supreme courts." Law and Society Rev. 4 (November): 271-291.
——— and K. N. VINES (1973) State Court Systems. Englewood Cliffs: Prentice-Hall.
HARE, A. P., E. F. BORGATTA and R. F. BALES (1965) Small Groups. New York: Alfred A. Knopf.
HOMANS, G. (1950) The Human Group. New York: Harcourt, Brace.
HORNEY, K. (1950) Neurosis and Human Growth. New York: Norton.
——— (1945) Our Inner Conflicts. New York: Norton.
——— (1937) The Neurotic Personality of Our Time. New York: Norton.
HOWARD, J. (1968) "On the fluidity of judicial choice." Amer. Pol. Sci. Rev. 62 (March): 43-56.
JANIS, I. L. (1972) Victims of Groupthink. Boston: Houghton-Mifflin.
KOONTZ, H. and C. O'DONNELL (1972) Principles of Management: An Analysis of Managerial Functions. New York: McGraw-Hill.
KORT, F. (1962) "Content analysis of judicial opinions and rules of law," pp. 133-197 in G. Schubert (ed.) Judicial Decision-Making. New York: Free Press.
KRISLOV, S. (1963) "Power and coalition in a nine-man body." Amer. Behavioral Scientist 6 (April): 24-26.
McELWAIN, E. (1949) "The business of the supreme court as conducted by chief justice Hughes." Harvard Law Rev. 63 (November): 5-26.

MASON, A. T. (1964) William Howard Taft: Chief Justice. New York: Simon & Schuster.
MILLER, A. S. and D. S. SASTRI (1973) "Secrecy and the supreme court: on the need for piercing the red velour curtain." Buffalo Law Rev. 22 (Spring): 799-823.
MURPHY, W. F. (1964) Elements of Judicial Strategy. Chicago: Univ. of Chicago Press.
NAGEL, S. S. (1969) The Legal Process from a Behavioral Perspective. Homewood, Ill.: Dorsey Press.
––– (1961) "Political party affiliation and judges' decisions." Amer. Pol. Sci. Rev. 55: 842-850.
SCHUBERT, G. A. (1965) The Judicial Mind. Evanston: Northwestern Univ. Press.
––– (1959) Quantitative Analysis of Judicial Behavior. Glencoe: Free Press.
SCIGLIANO, R. (1971) The Supreme Court and the Presidency. New York: Free Press.
SHAPIRO, M. (1968) "The House and the federal role: a computer simulation of roll-call voting." Amer. Pol. Sci. Rev. 62 (June): 494-517.
SHERIF, M. (1947) "Group influences upon the formation of norms and attitudes," in T. M. Newcomb and E. L. Hartley (eds.) Readings in Social Psychology. New York: Holt, Rinehart & Winston.
SLATER, P. E. (1955) "Role differentiation in small groups." Amer. Soc. Rev. 20: 300-310.
SNYDER, E. (1958) "The supreme court as a small group." Social Forces 36 (March): 232-238.
SPAETH, H. J. (1962) "Judicial power as a variable motivating supreme court behavior." Midwest J. of Pol. Sci. 6 (May): 54-82.
SPRAGUE, J. D. (1968) Voting Patterns of the United States Supreme Court: Cases in Federalism 1889-1959. Indianapolis: Bobbs-Merrill.
ULMER, S. S. (1971) Courts as Small and Not So Small Groups. New York: General Learning Press.
––– (1971a) "Earl Warren and the *Brown* decision," J. of Politics 33: 689-702.
–– (1963) "Leadership in the Michigan Supreme Court," pp. 13-28 in G. Schubert (ed.) Judicial Decision-Making. Glencoe: Free Press.
––– (1962) "The political party variable in the Michigan Supreme Court." J. of Public Law 11: 352-362.
VERBA, S. (1961) Small Groups and Political Behavior. Princeton: Princeton Univ. Press.

APPENDIX A

I. States Providing Permanent Tenure for the Chief Justice

    1. New York   California
    2. Pennsylvania   New Jersey
    3. Wisconsin

II. States Providing Long Tenures of Office for the Chief Justice

    4. Colorado   1951-1961
    5. Colorado   1962-1971
    6. Florida   1951-1961
    7. Florida   1962-1971
    8. Michigan
    9. Nevada   Oregon
  10. Oklahoma
  11. Washington

III. States Providing Short Tenures for the Chief Justice

  12. Illinois   1953-1960
  13. Illinois   1960-1971
  14. South Dakota   1952-1963
  15. South Dakota   1964-1971

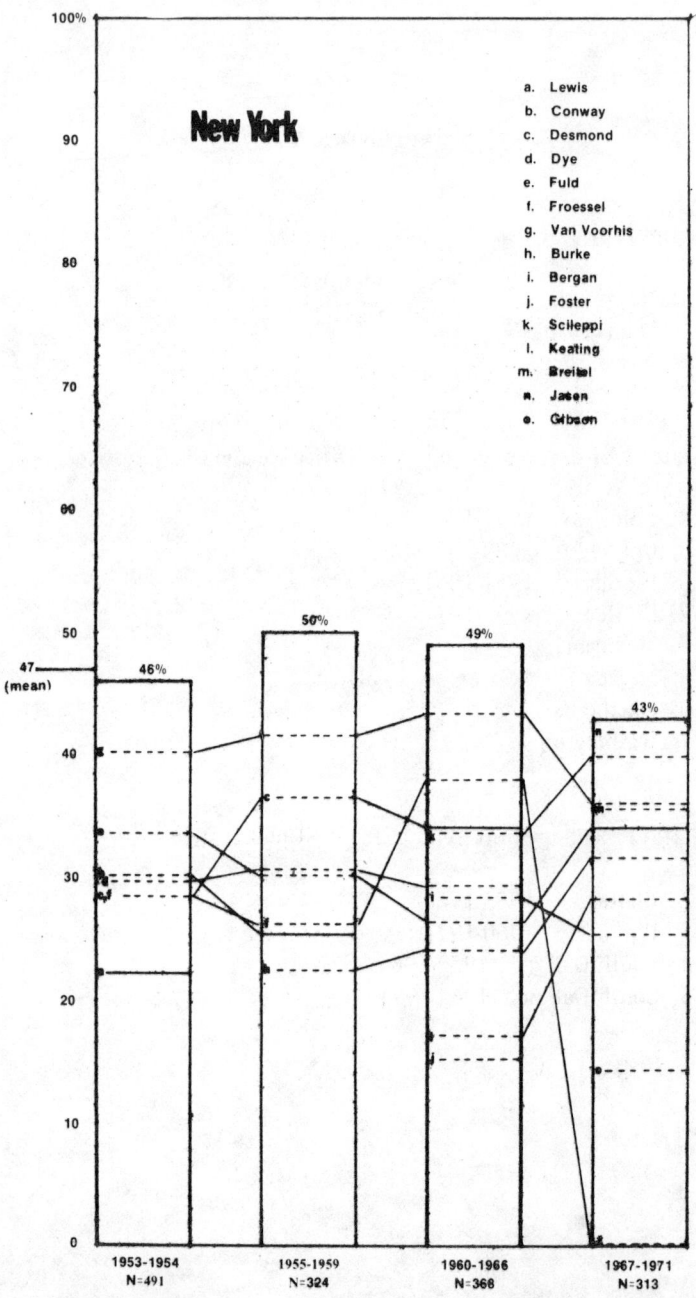

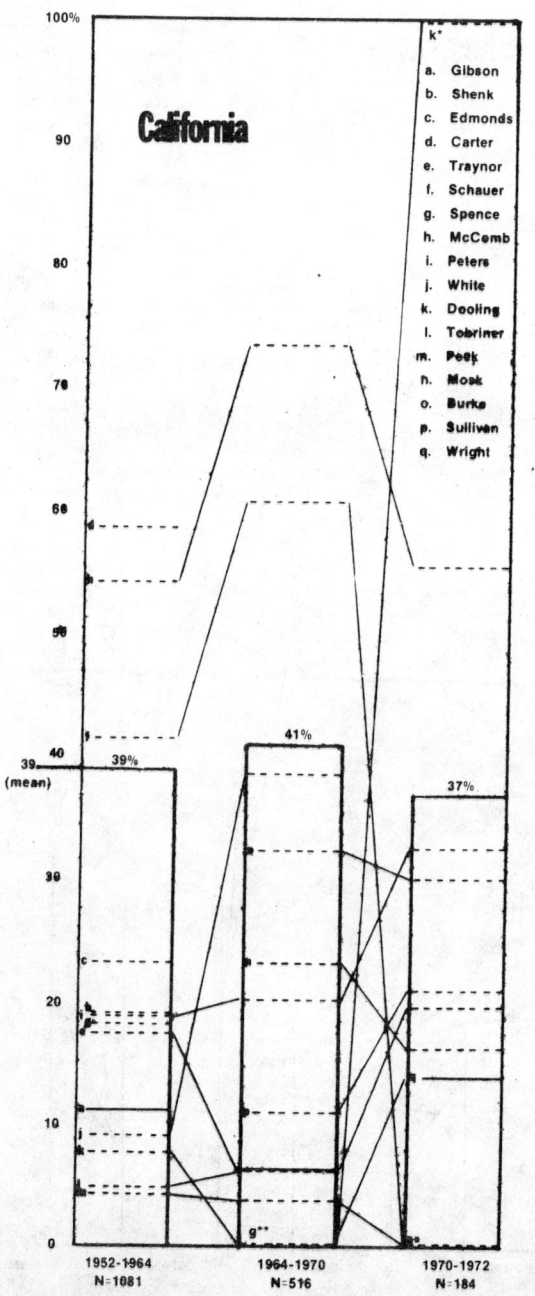

[29]

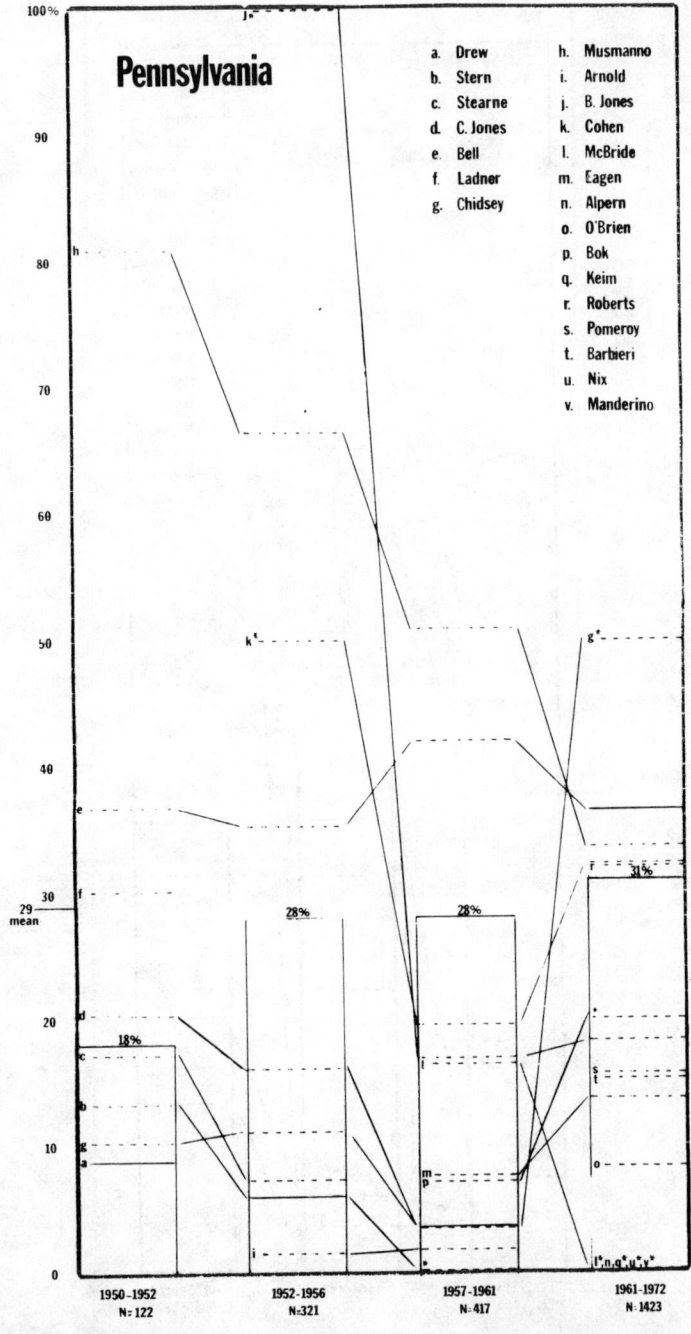

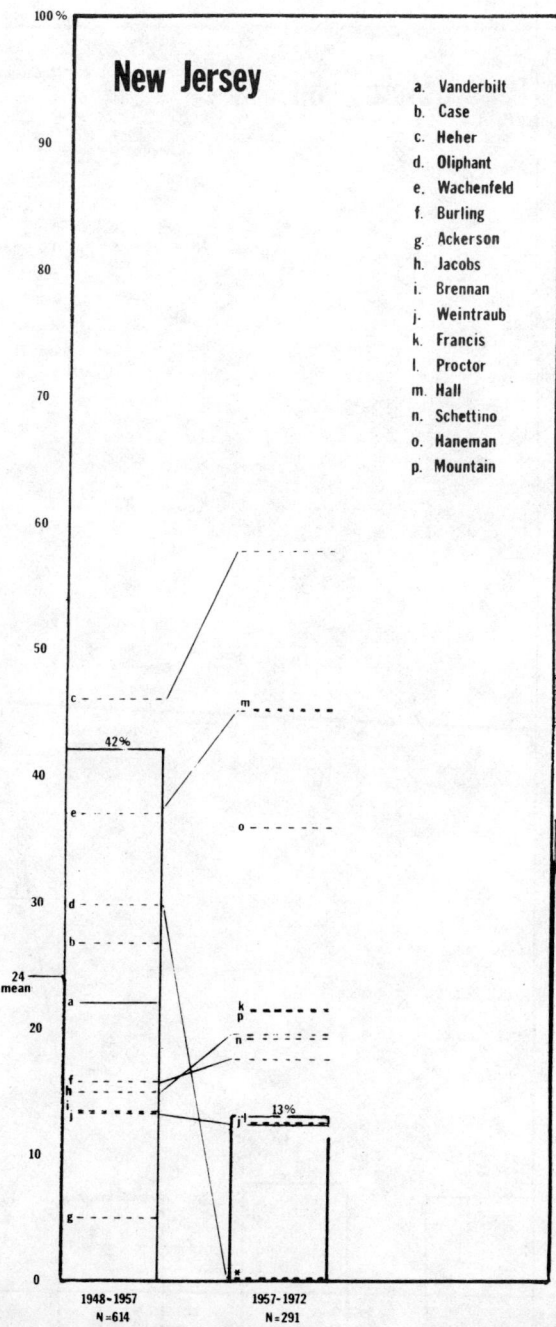

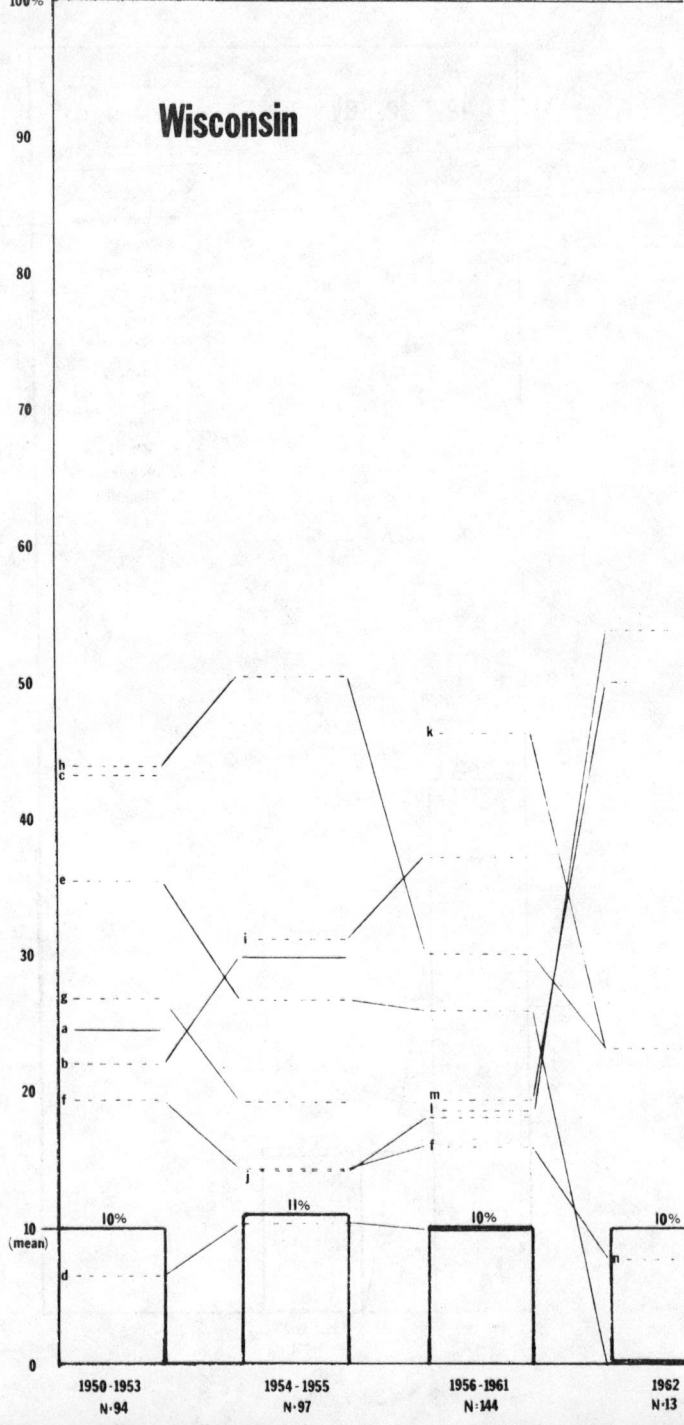

a.	Fritz	k.	T. Fairchild
b.	E. Fairchild	l.	Hallows
c.	Hughes	m.	Dieterich
d.	Martin	n.	Gordon
e.	Broadfoot	o.	Wilkie
f.	Brown	p.	Beilfuss
g.	Gehl	q.	Heffernan
h.	Currie	r.	Hanley
i.	Steinle	s.	C. Hansen
j.	Wingert	t.	R. Hansen

[34]

A—4

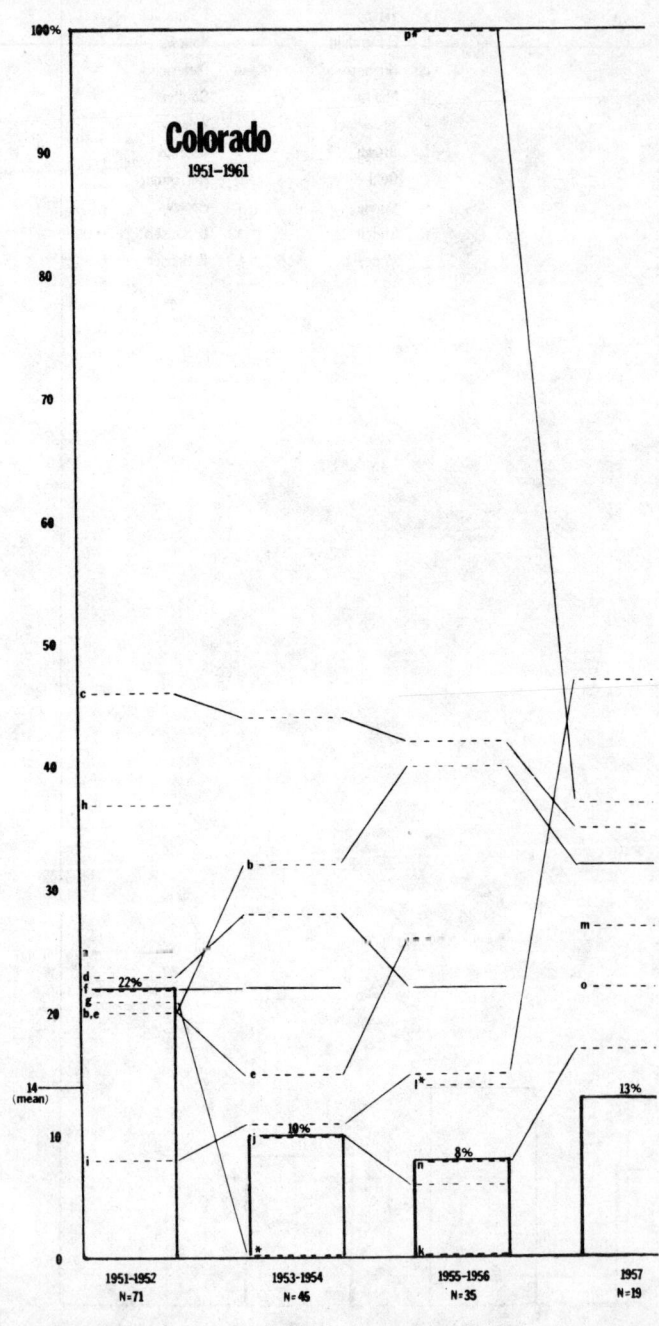

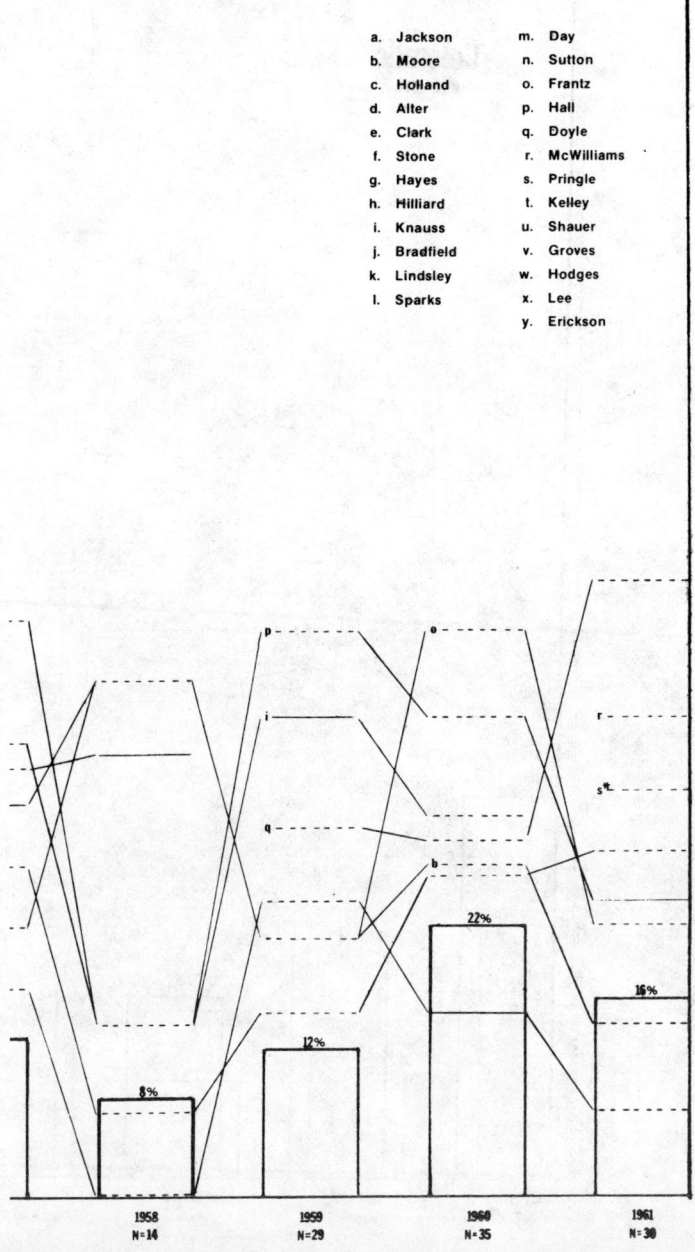

[36]

A—5

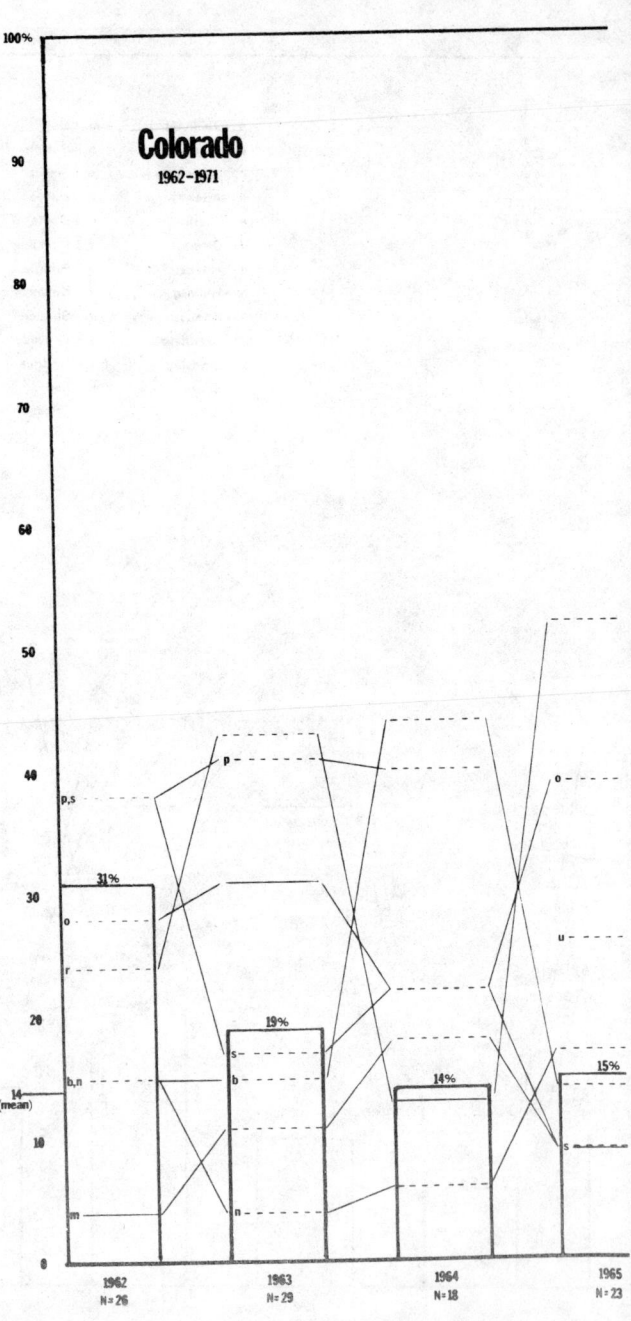

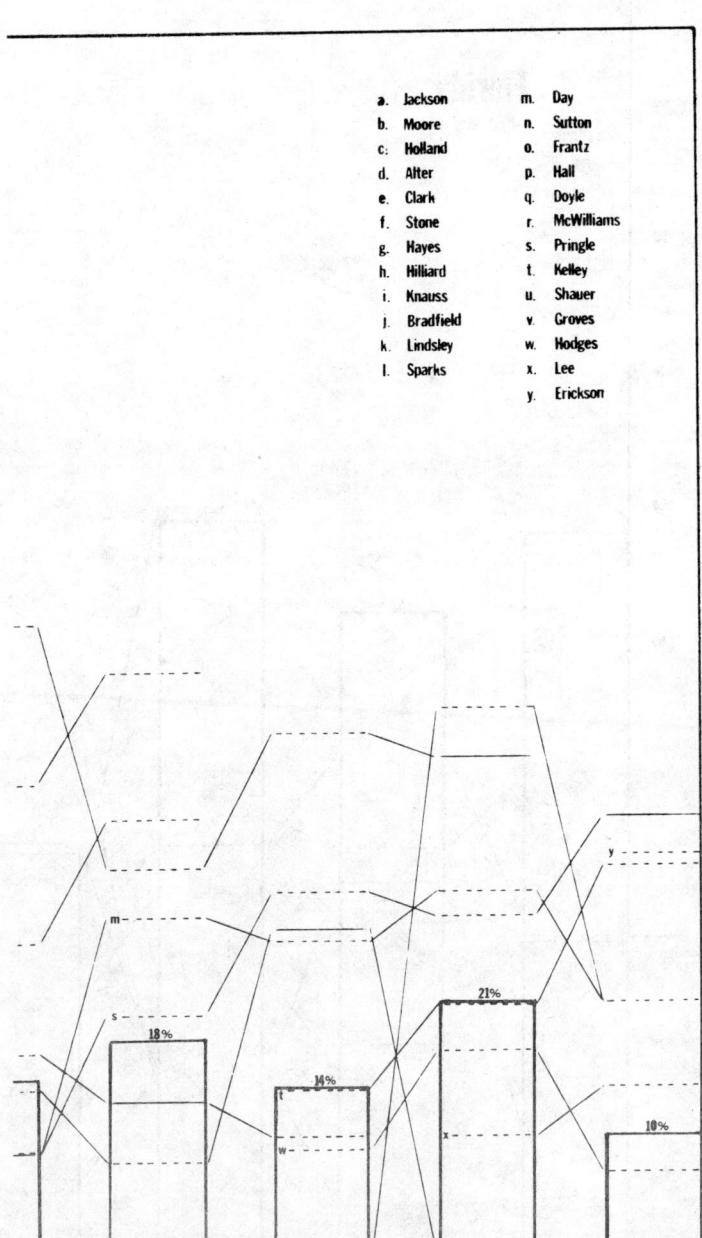

[38] **A—6**

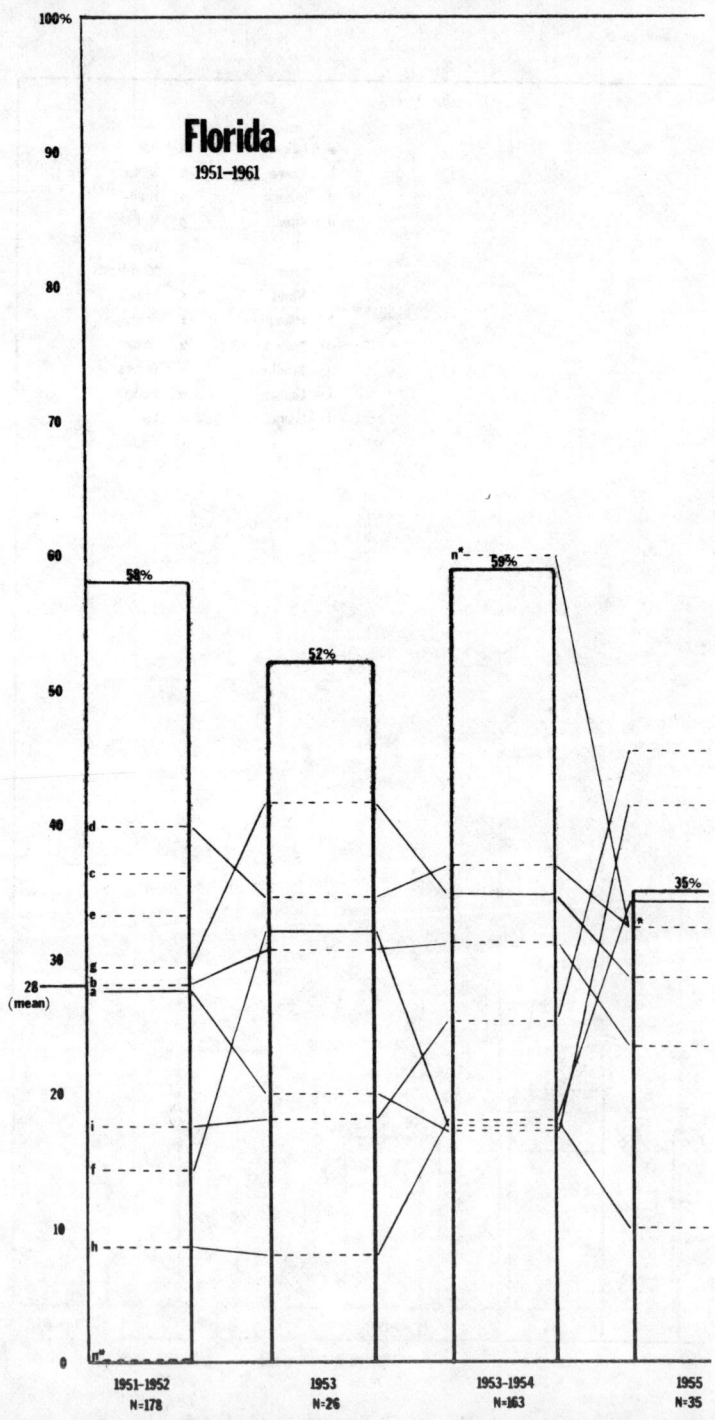

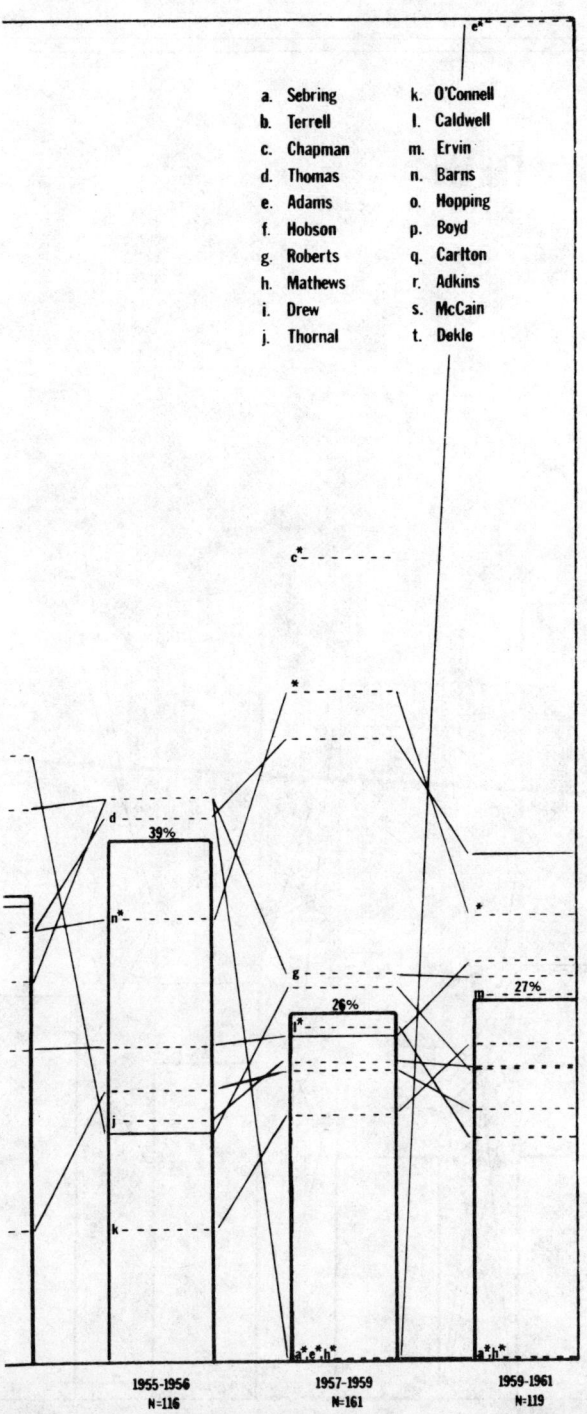

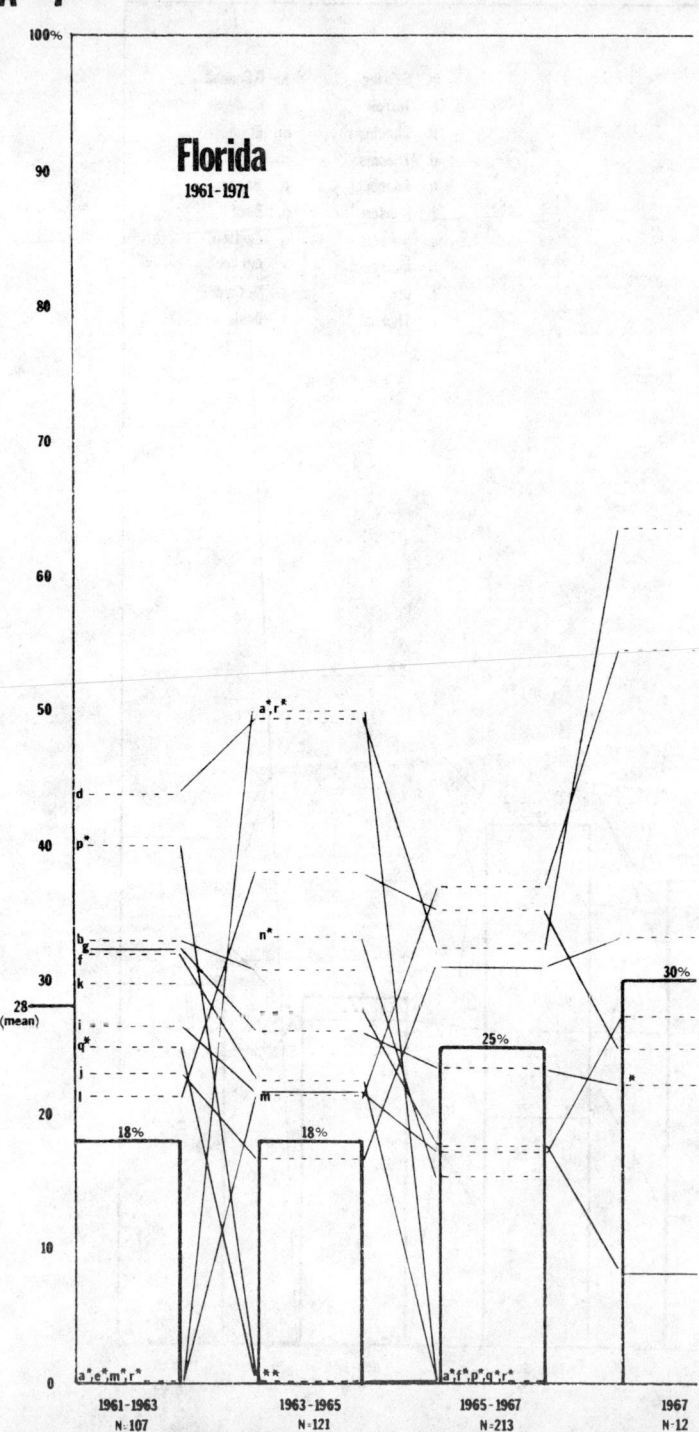

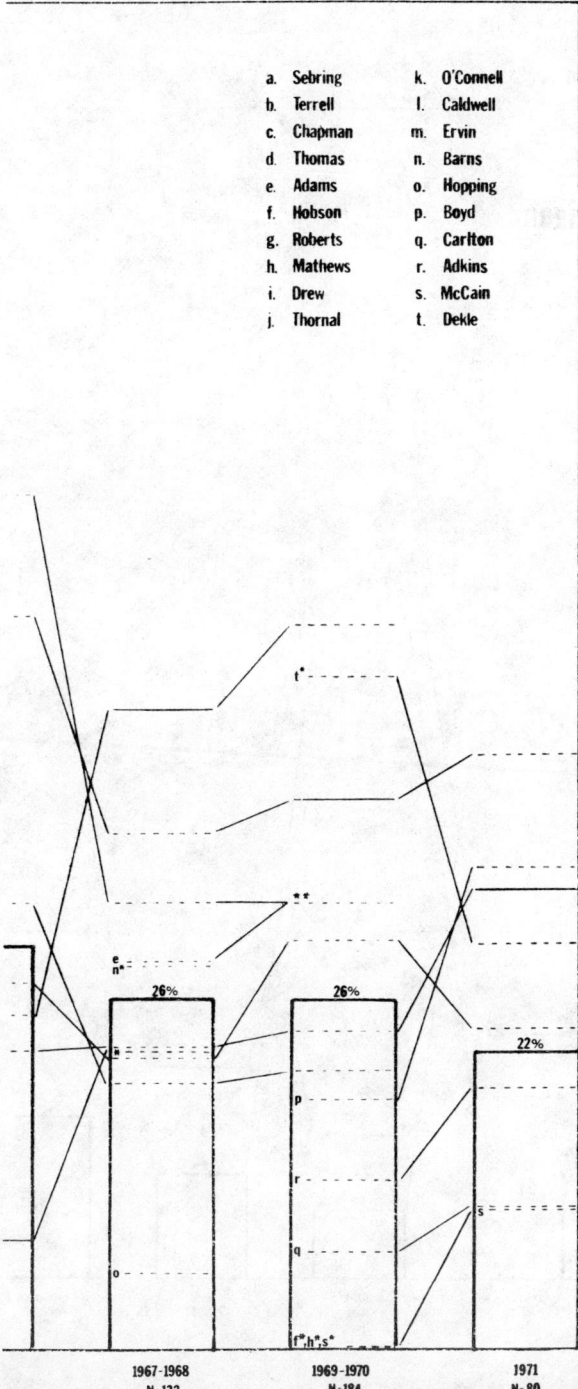

A—8

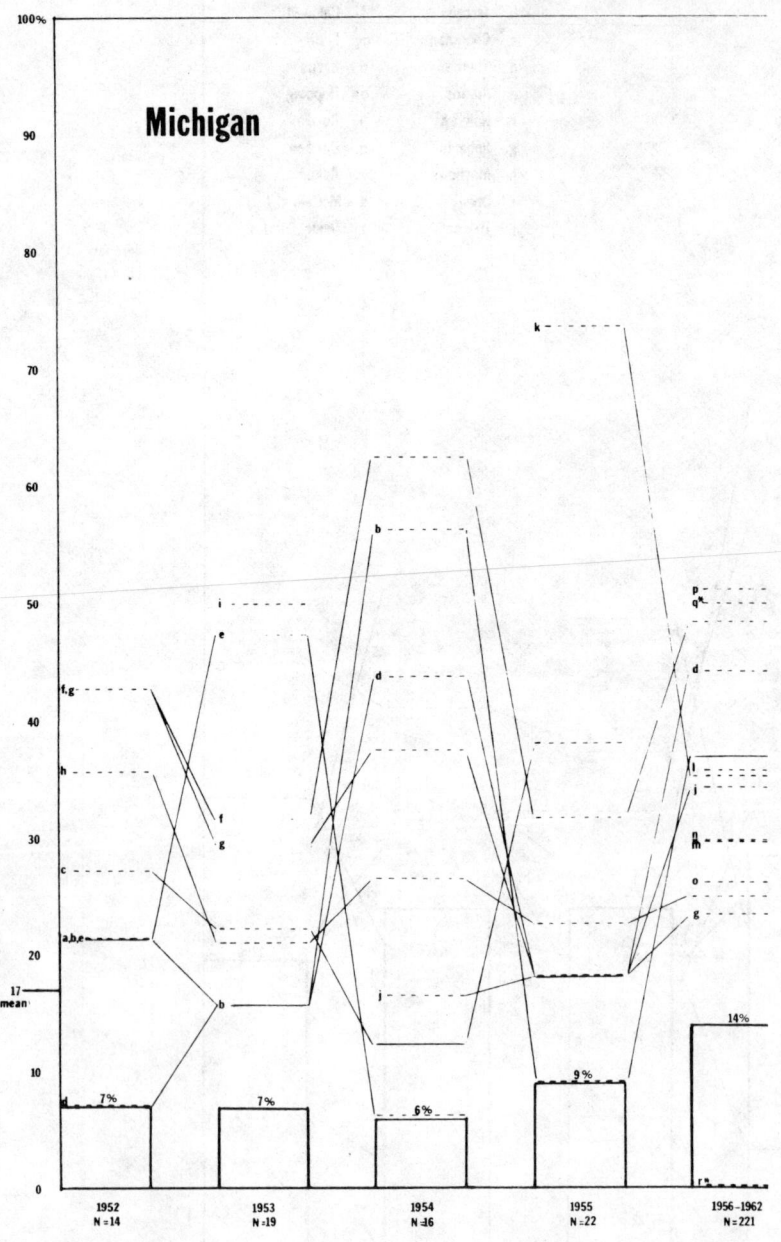

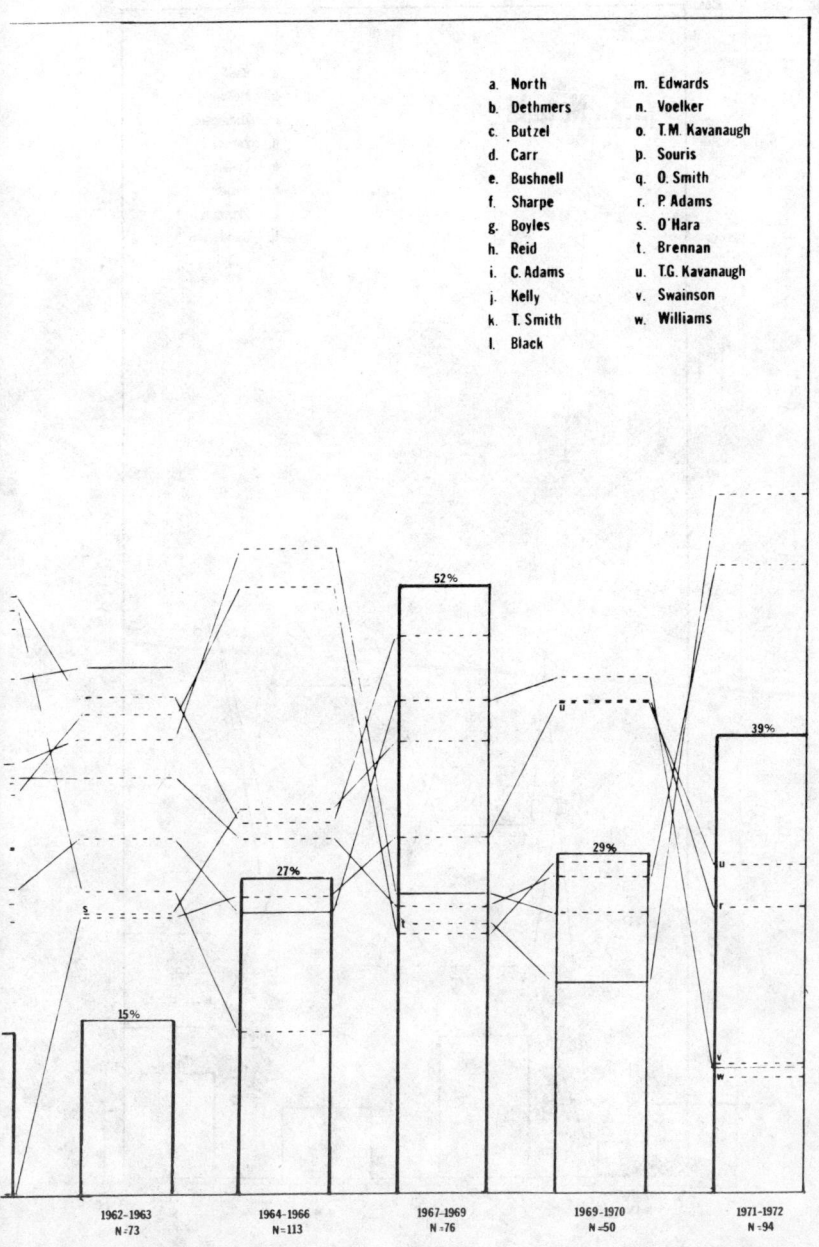

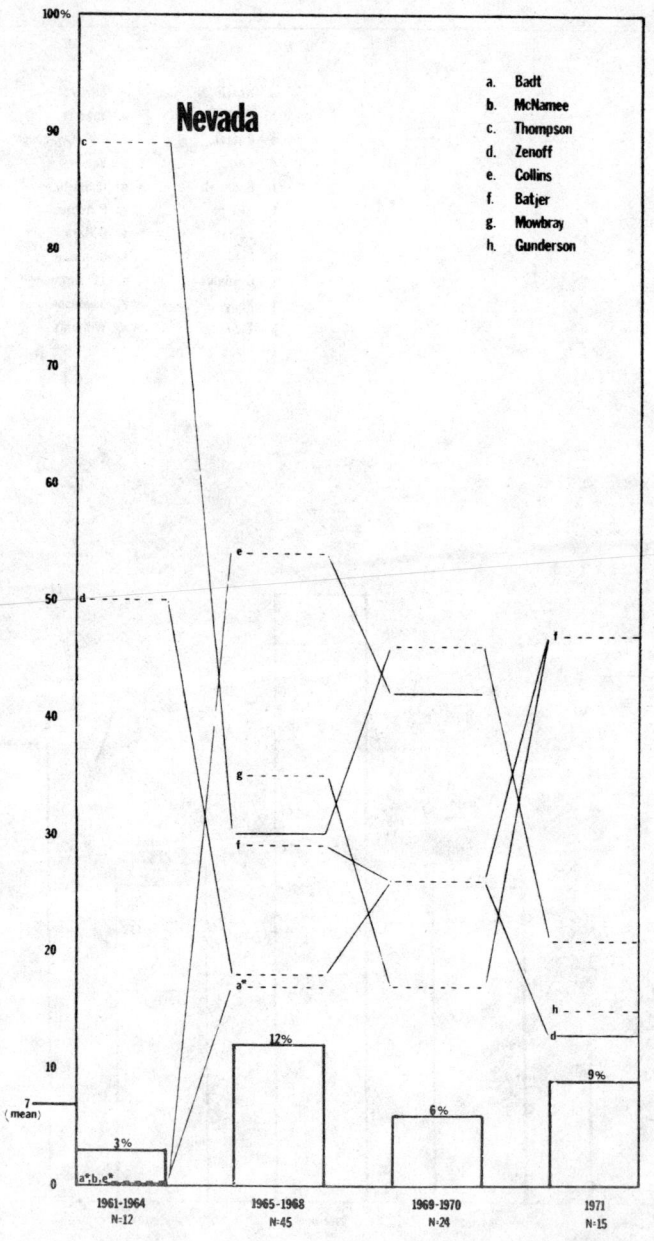

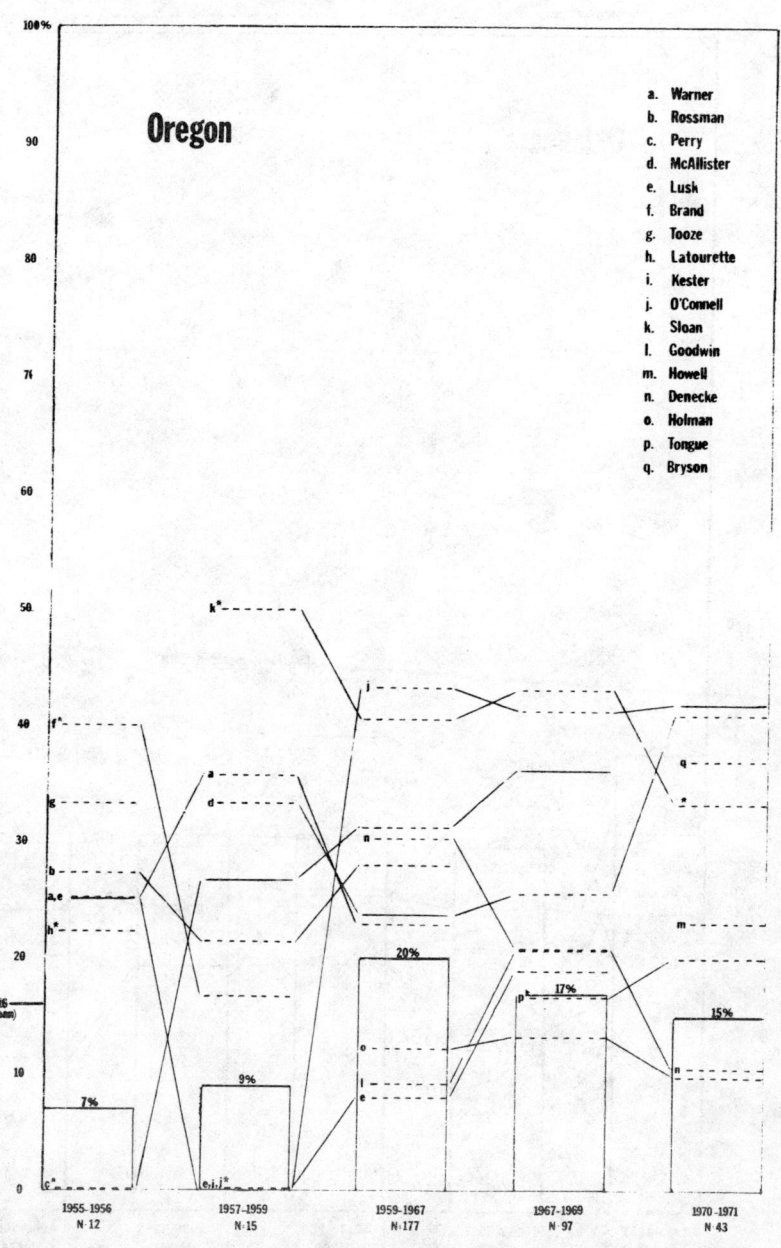

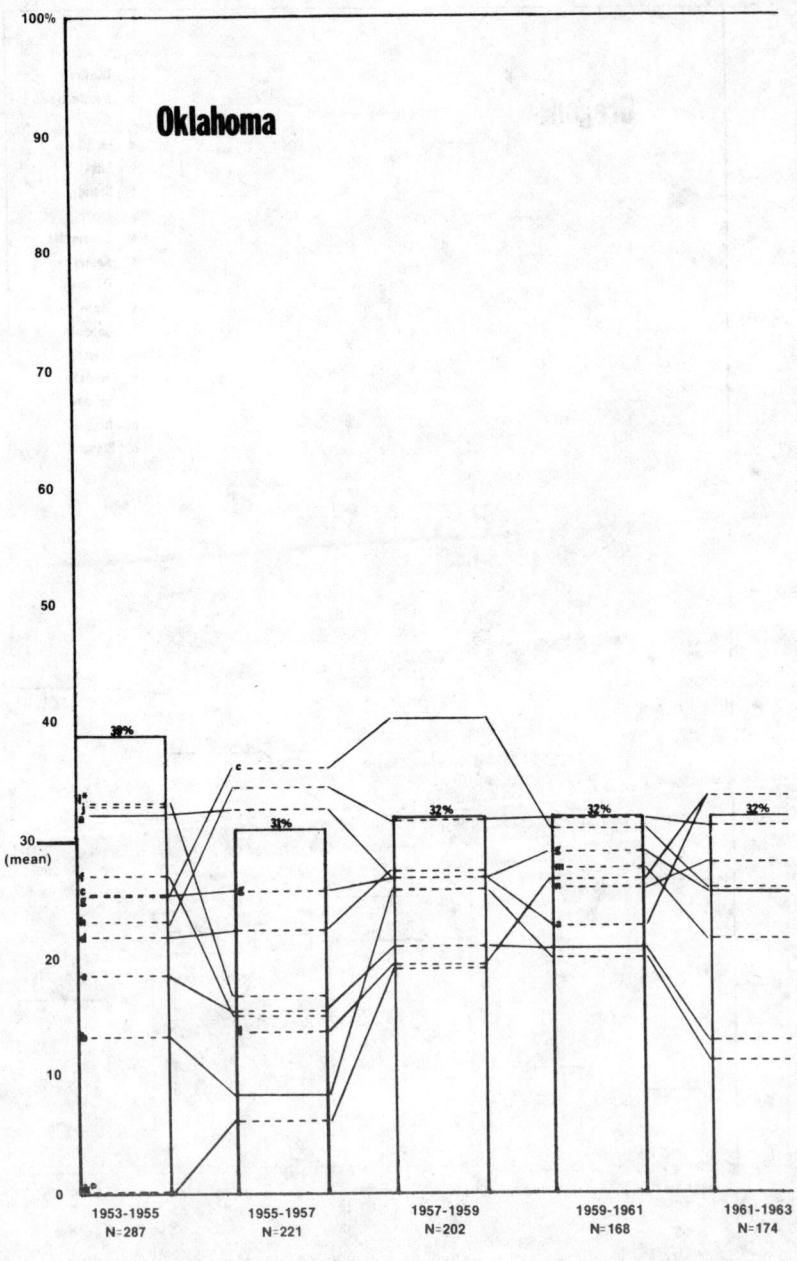

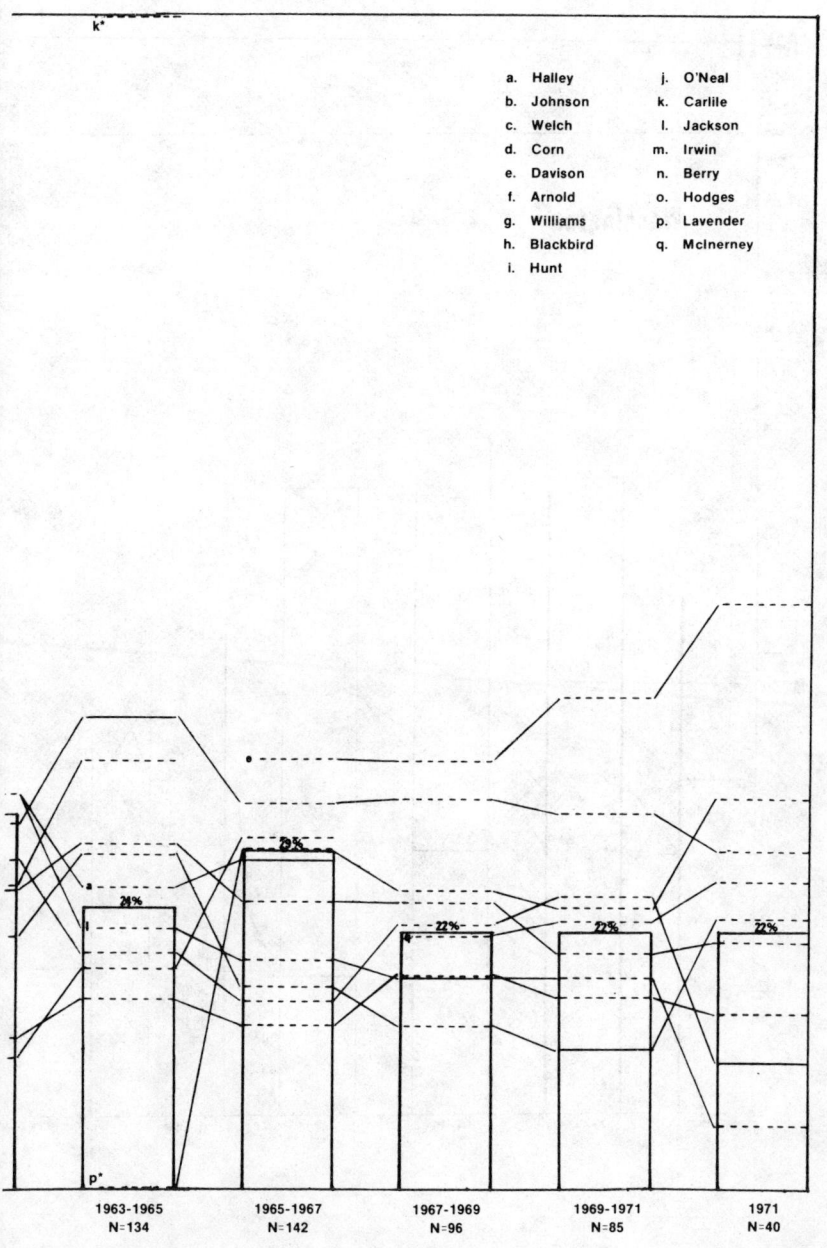

[48]

A—11

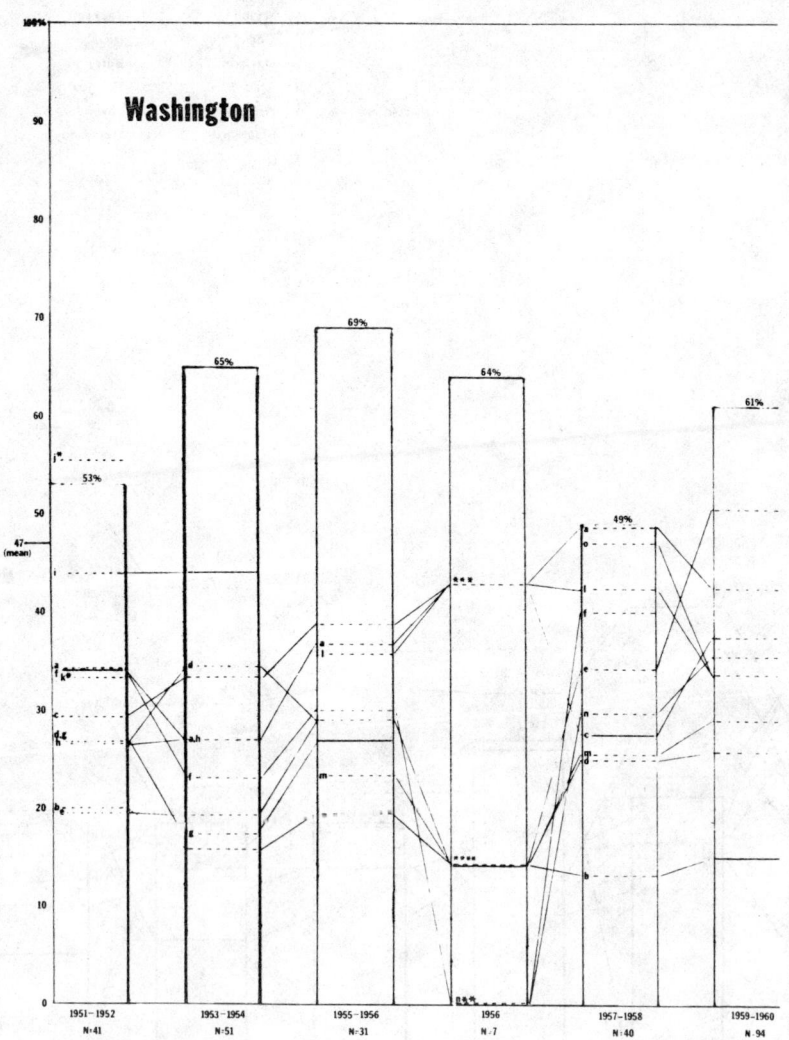

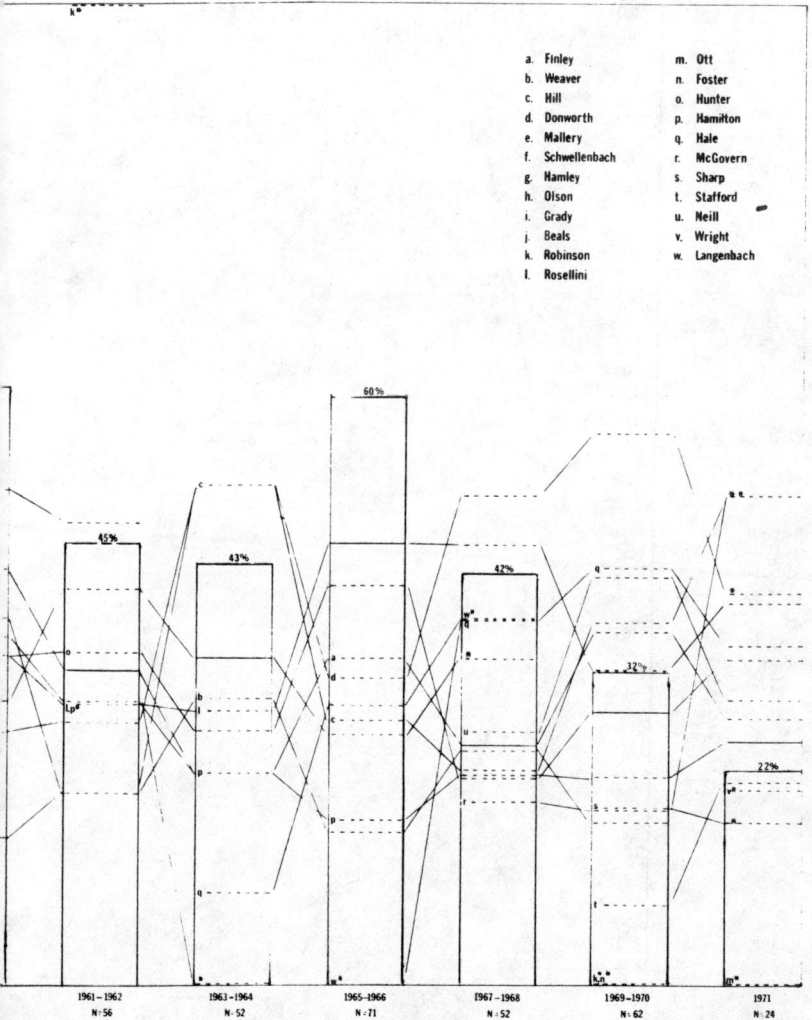

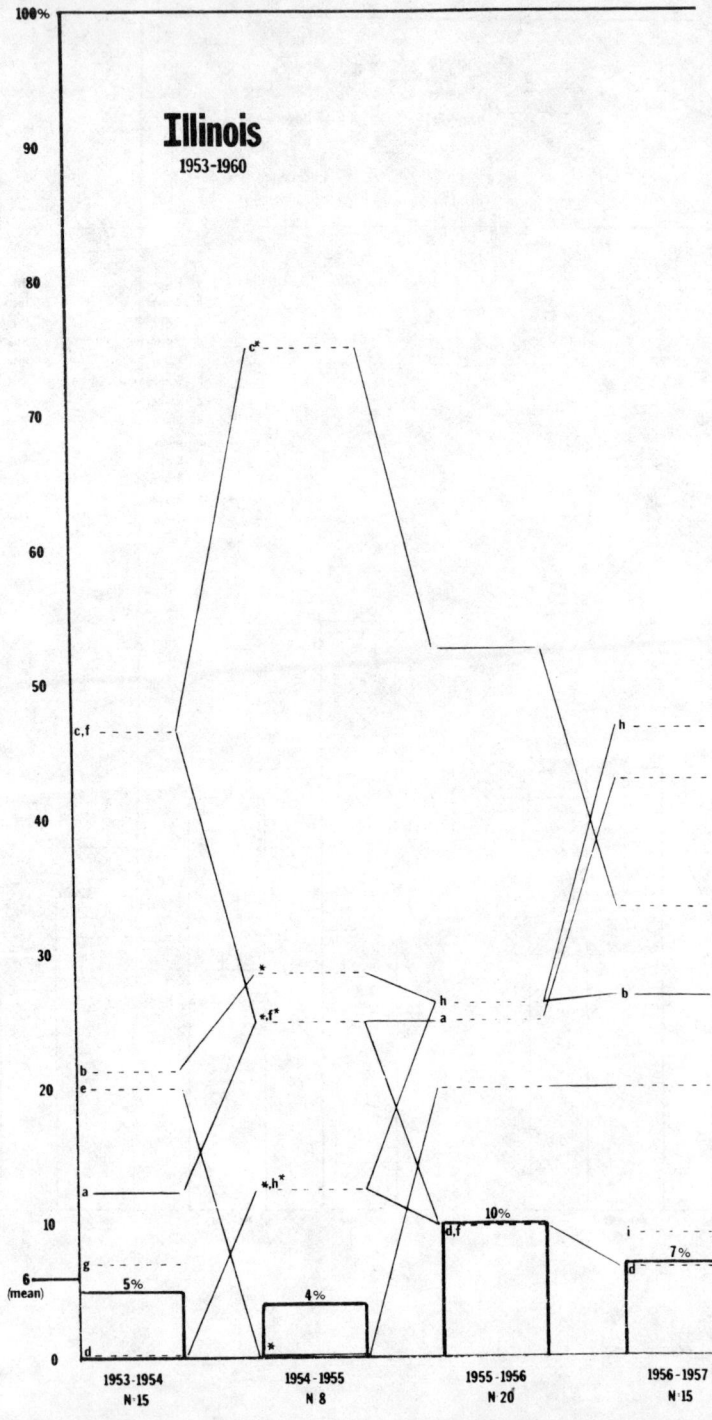

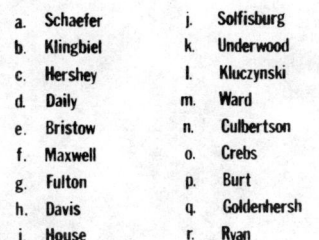
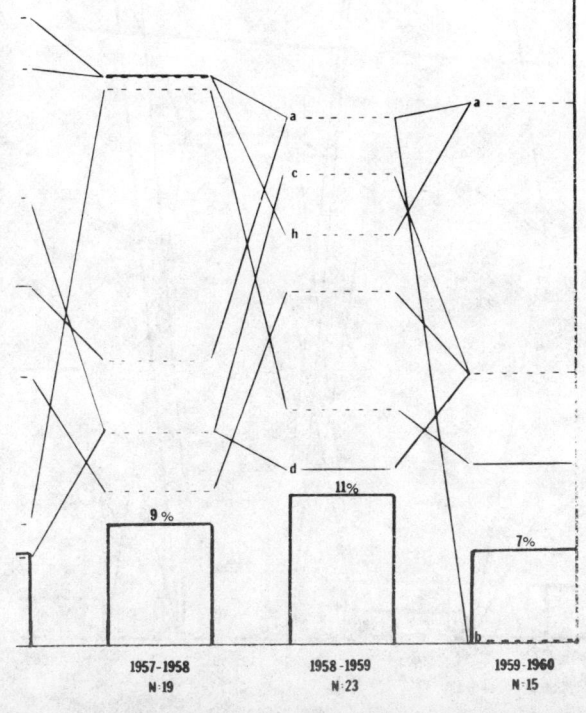

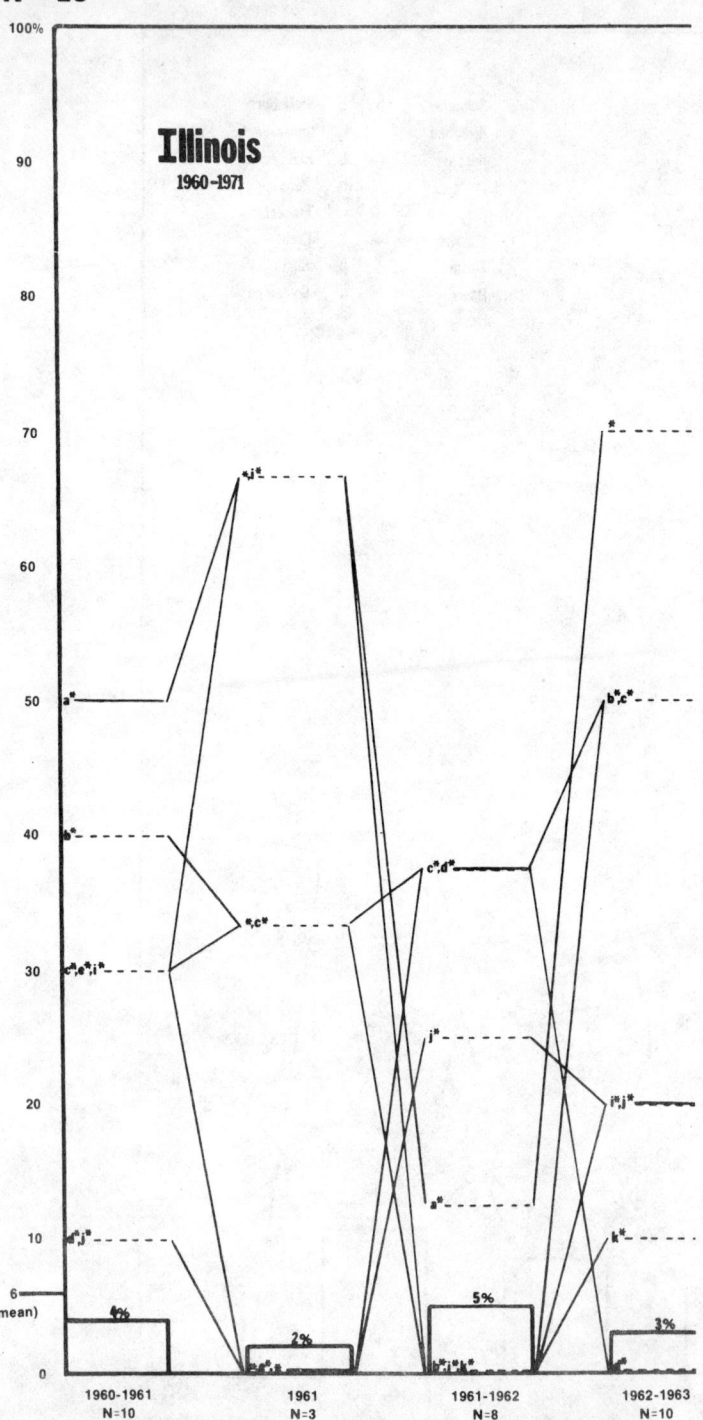

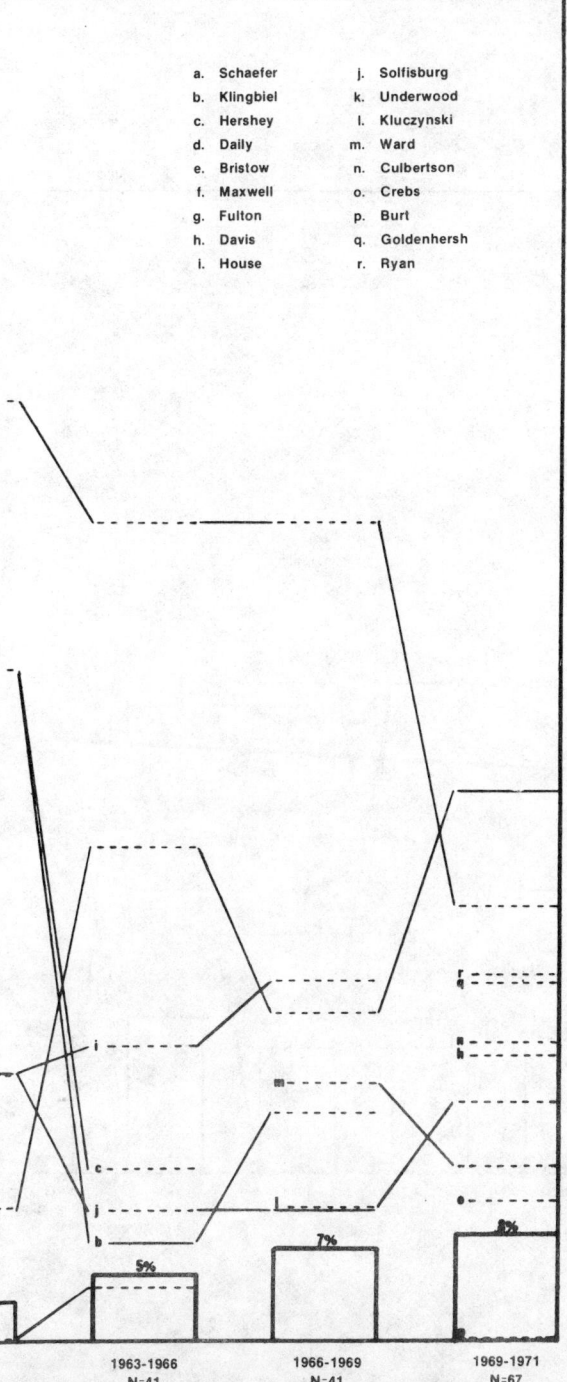

[54]

A—14

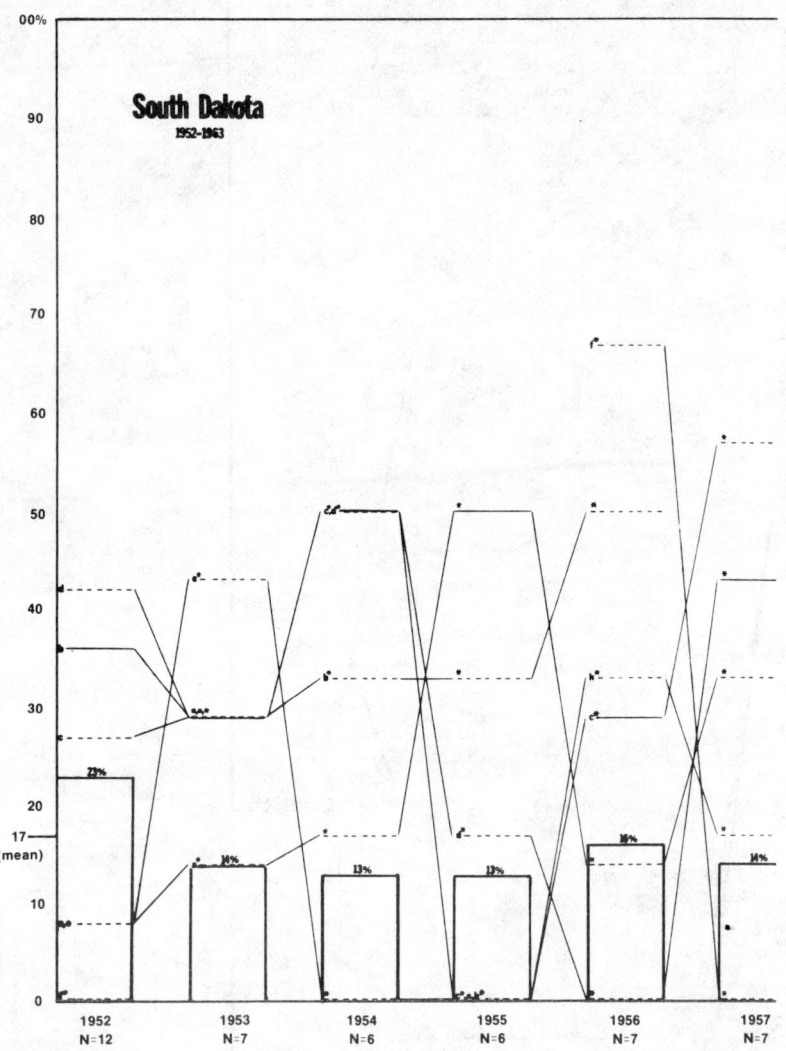

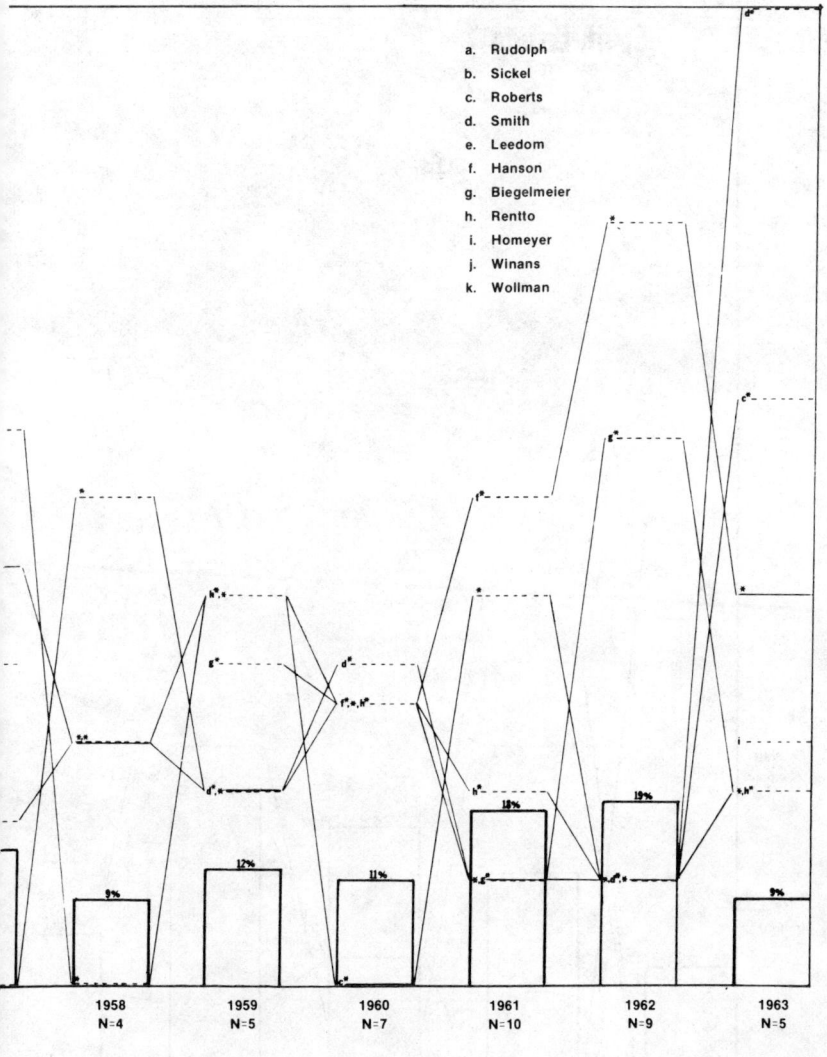

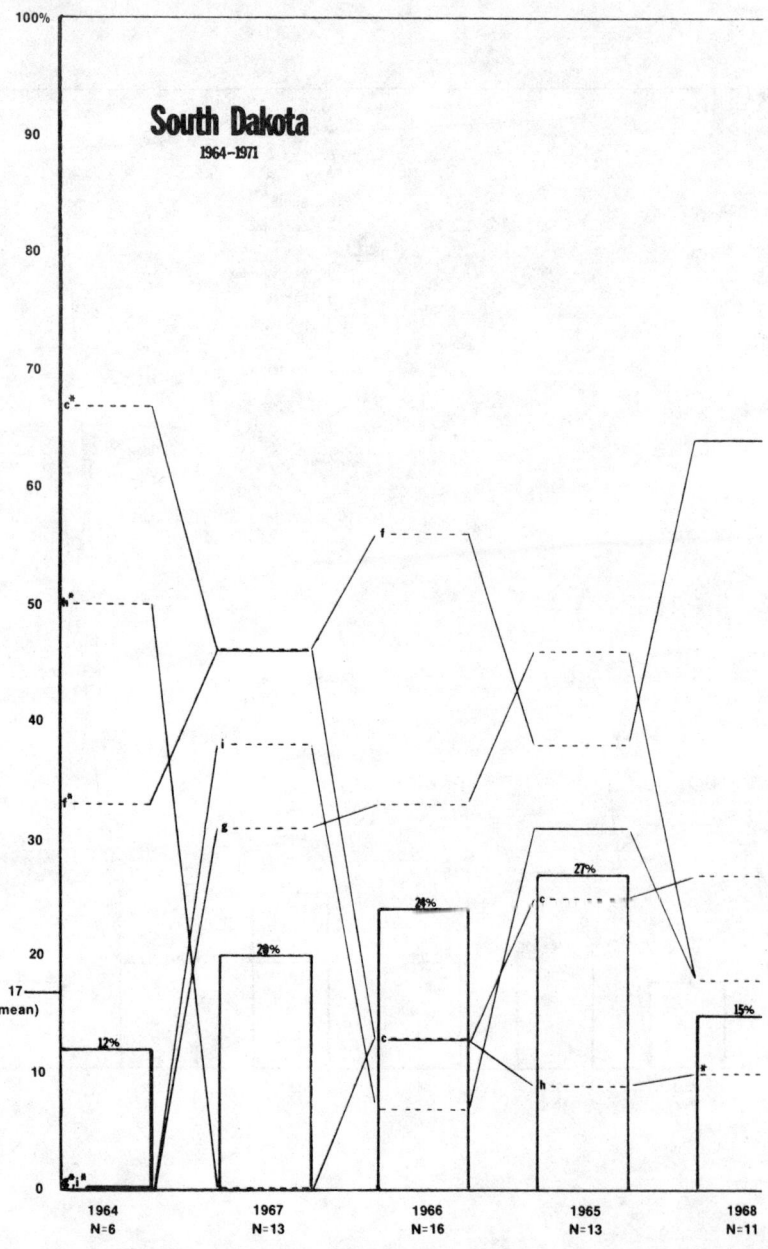

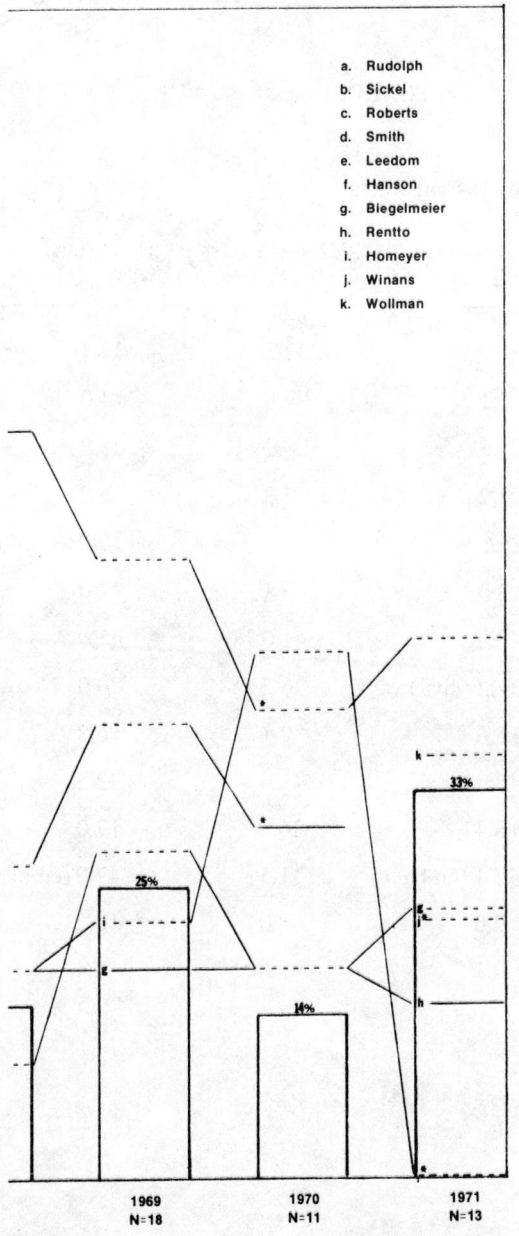

a. Rudolph
b. Sickel
c. Roberts
d. Smith
e. Leedom
f. Hanson
g. Biegelmeier
h. Rentto
i. Homeyer
j. Winans
k. Wollman

APPENDIX B

Comparison of State Court Dissent Rates

	Canon and Jaros 1961-1967	Glick and Vines 1966	This Study 1951-1972
California	31.7	32.3	39.4
Colorado	7.1	9.8	14.0
Florida	21.5	28.2	28.2
Illinois	7.2	7.2	6.0
Michigan	26.2	46.5	17.0
New Jersey	12.0	7.1	24.0
New York	49.0	41.0	47.0
Oklahoma	31.2 (civil)	26.5	30.0
Oregon	11.6	9.1	16.3
Pennsylvania	40.3	41.0	29.2
South Dakota	18.4	24.3	17.0
Washington	48.4 (en banc)	11.5	47.0 (en banc)
Wisconsin	9.6	8.0	10.2
Nevada	9.1	9.8	7.4

CRAIG ROBB DUCAT is associate professor of political science at Northern Illinois University. He earned his B.A. at Syracuse University and his M.A. and Ph.D. degrees at the University of Minnesota. His published work deals with judicial decision-making, the U.S. Constitution, and governmental processes.

VICTOR EUGENE FLANGO, assistant professor of political science at Northern Illinois University, received degrees from Indiana University of Pennsylvania and the University of Hawaii. Dr. Flango's articles on judicial behavior and criminal justice policies have been published in the American Journal of Political Science, Comparative Judicial Behavior, *and* Administrative Science Quarterly.